ROAST

THE HOME MEZCAL-MAKING GUIDE TO CRAFTING DELIGHTFUL TIPPLES WITH TRADITIONAL OAXACAN METHODS

DAVID DUMONT

CONTENTS

Dedicated to my remarkable mother, with whom I roasted on many a winter's evening.

INTRODUCTION

> *Para todo mal, mezcal, y para todo bien también.*
>
> *For everything bad, mezcal, and for everything good as well.*
>
> — MEXICAN PROVERB

> *Big things have small beginnings.*
>
> — T.E. LAWRENCE IN *LAWRENCE OF ARABIA* AND DAVID
> IN *PROMETHEUS*

Probably one of the best places to taste *mezcal* is in its traditional production center—Oaxaca in southwestern Mexico. Located in a lush valley surrounded by soaring mountains, Oaxaca City is a kaleidoscope of vivid colors, where the tall spires of historic churches rise above an eclectic mix of Spanish Colonial and traditional architecture. As you enter the city, you can see that mezcal-making is a thriving local industry; rows of agave, the primary ingredient, line its access roads. In the city itself, stalls selling unique versions of the local elixir jostle for roadside space, with many mezcal distilleries, or *palenques,* displaying the huge stone wheels used to crush the plants. Each stall sells its own version of mezcal and many have private tasting rooms for curious drinkers to take their first sips, while mezcal connoisseurs can sample different variations of these traditional spirits.

Mezcal, stored in a range of odd-shaped glass bottles, is also available in watering holes around the city—just as it is in several major U.S. cities, including New York, Los Angeles, Washington DC, San Francisco, and Austin. Tiny, alluring tasting rooms, their walls hung with cultural artifacts and paintings, showcase everything mezcal.

These spirits have singular spicy or smoky, yet sweet flavors that are sometimes enhanced by the addition of flavoring ingredients during the final distillation. These are selected at the producer's discretion and can be anything from spices, fresh herbs, and tropical fruits to a chicken or turkey breast smoked over the still. Only limited quantities of mezcal made the traditional way are available. However, increasingly popular barrel aging methods are producing mellower, smoother versions of the drink.

The best way to enjoy mezcal—with its exotic attributes—is to imbibe it along with the deliciously different local Oaxacan cuisine. Tourists may attend festivals where people in bright folk outfits demonstrate their cultural dances for crowds gathered to eat, drink, and be merry.

WHAT IS MEZCAL?

Mezcal is a distilled spirit made from the sweet sap found in the thickened stems, or *piñas,* of agave plants. In Oaxaca, where it is known as maguey, it has been produced since 400 B.C. Today, this largely handcrafted, fiery spirit is also made in eight other Mexican states (Admin, 2019; Gonzalez, 2022).

Several of the 150 species and varieties of agave growing in Mexico are used to produce this traditional drink (Todd and Diane, 2011). Each one creates a unique mezcal with its own flavors and aromas. Some of the better-known mezcals produced are bottled with a worm that is actually the larva of a moth that feeds on the plants. The worm is not required to produce mezcal, however it is often added to create interest for marketing purposes.

The word *mezcal* is derived from the Aztec word *mexcalli,* which means "baked or cooked agave," and refers to its traditional production methods. Turning agave nectar into mezcal begins by roasting the piñas in an underground earthen or brick oven for several days, a process that confers to the drink its smoky flavor and somewhat charred aftertastes, after which they are crushed, either by hand or by a giant stone pulled by a horse or donkey to release the juice. This juice is collected in large wooden vats and fermented using natural, airborne yeasts. It is later distilled two or three times in a copper or clay still (Gonzalez, 2022). Various *esculents* are sometimes hung in the still during the final distillation to add unique flavor notes. The resulting liquid is mezcal. Because many people make mezcal in small quantities, the variety of flavors and aromas is extensive.

Mezcal that has not been subject to aging is called *joven,* or young. Mezcal that has been aged in wooden barrels (usually for two to twelve months) bears the poetic title of *reposado*, best translated here as "rested". The aging process and evocative name also apply to tequila. Both spirits, in their resting phase, acquire from their barrels very special characteristics and are often amber-colored (Eby, 2023). Longer aging produces a mezcal dubbed *añejo*, or mature. *Añejo* has a darker color similar to that of whisky.

Mezcal Versus Tequila: What's the Difference?

While the terms tequila and mezcal both describe agave spirits, they are not interchangeable. Mezcal refers to a wide variety of spirits distilled from agave plants, which includes tequila. This is much the same as Chardonnay being a type of wine. Whereas only Blue Weber agave is used to make tequila, any type of agave can be harvested to make mezcal, including both wild and cultivated varieties (Eby, 2023). Blue Weber agave grows only in certain parts of Mexico.

There are additional differences between the spirits. To make mezcal, the piñas are roasted in an oven in the ground; to make tequila, they are steamed in an above-ground brick oven or a modern autoclave, which is similar to a giant pressure cooker. This results in more uniform flavors and makes it easier to produce tequila commercially, which is why it's more common than mezcal on American bar shelves. Tequila is more likely to be aged than mezcal and if so, for longer.

ORIGINS OF MEZCAL

Ancestors of today's Mexicans once produced a fermented drink called *pulque*, derived from the sugar-rich sap of agave flower stalks. This low-alcohol drink was widely consumed, and variations of it are still made across Mexico. The Spanish introduced copper stills and distillation methods to the region around four hundred years ago, enabling the production of the first mezcal, and local lore is ripe with colorful details (Gonzalez, 2022).

In one tale a Zapotec Indian, looking for a source of sustenance after a hurricane, was attracted by a strong, but not unpleasant smell. An agave plant had been struck by lightning, and its roasted flesh, with its unexpectedly sweet flavor, proved to be a culinary delight. The happy man took it back to his community, which began roasting the plants to produce a natural candy. When the Spanish arrived with their copper stills, they discovered that the roasted agaves eaten by the Zapotecs had a high sugar content and decided to try distilling the juice from the roasted piña. Whatever its precise origins, mezcal was born.

CATEGORIES OF MEZCAL

The Consejo Regulador de Mezcal (CRM) recognizes three legal categories of the spirit. Each one is defined by the methods and equipment producers used to make their version of it. The categories are (McKirdy, 2020):

- The word *mezcal* generally refers to spirits produced by means of industrial methods and high-tech modern equipment, including autoclaves, stainless steel fermentation vats, and modern stills.
- The term *artisanal* applies to mezcal made via traditional production methods and with limited output. Pit ovens are used for roasting, while wooden tanks, hollowed-out stones or tree trunks, and animal skins may be used during fermentation. Stills are either made of clay or copper.
- The adjective *ancestral* honors a type of mezcal painstakingly crafted just as it was hundreds of years ago. Only clay pots and fire are used to distill it. Very few producers are prepared and equipped to make this category of mezcal.

FLAVORS AND AROMAS

As we have seen, one category of mezcal comes from state-of-the-art facilities that bear little resemblance to what the Zapotec hero of the earlier told mescal-origin story would ever recognize. However, the other two types of mezcal are artisanal creations from the numerous distilleries located in small villages and faithfully applying methods handed down through generations. Each village has its special way of distilling mezcal, the flavor of which is influenced by the type of agave used, the flavorings added during fermentation, and even the minerality of the village's water supply. This creates drinks that have a unique identity. Some boast flavors that range from smoky to smooth or sweet. Others are muscular spirits that take your breath away. Nevertheless, mezcal is easy to sip, vaguely reminiscent of tequila but with a greater complexity of flavors and aroma.

Like fine wines, mezcals are sometimes blended to create unusual drinks pleasantly suggestive of sun-dried vegetables, citrus, dried, or other fruit. They can have floral or earthy notes, tinged with the subtle scent of woodsmoke. Some mezcal flavors are reminiscent of pepper, fennel, jasmine, roasted figs, sweet potatoes, forest mushrooms, nuts, and spices. There are lingering aftertastes—charred tobacco, minerals, clay, dark chocolate, caramel, and spices.

UNLOCKING THE SECRETS OF MEZCAL

Perhaps you already enjoy drinking mezcal, which is gaining tremendous popularity in North America and elsewhere, or you have a growing fascination with the culture of Mexico. You may even be wondering whether it's possible to make your own agave drink, especially if you live in a region where the plant grows naturally, or if you have access to it or its piñas. Regardless, mezcal is more than simply another spirit. It's part of a rich cultural heritage and tradition spanning hundreds of years.

In this book, you'll find out about mezcal's cultural roots, as well as where and how it's produced in its native land. You'll also discover how to make it in your own backyard using simple, age-old methods combined with more modern technology and equipment.

You can do so while upholding mezcal's authenticity and respecting its historic cultural roots.

While the sheer variety of agave plants can seem overwhelming, this book will introduce you to the ones that are most suitable for mezcal production and explain how to grow these plants in your backyard or on your small farm, enabling you to produce a mezcal that will be as unique as you are.

Mezcal can always be combined with traditional Mexican foods in a special pairing not unlike that normally associated with fine wines. You'll discover exciting ways to pair mezcal with your best Mexican recipes for an unforgettable taste sensation. Drinking mezcal in moderation can also confer certain health benefits, which might be just the excuse you have been looking for!

This book will not only help you become proficient in making mezcal at home, but also give you a deeper appreciation and understanding of ancient cultural roots. You'll be equipped to produce high-quality, personalized mezcal and enjoy its rich taste sensations and multifaceted flavor profiles.

THE AGAVE LANDSCAPE

> *You can't fight the desert. You have to ride with it.*
>
> — LOUIS L'AMOUR

> *I cared for you in the wilderness, the land of drought.*
>
> — HOSEA 13:5, THE BIBLE

This chapter will introduce you to the statuesque, splendid agave, without which there would be no mezcal. Discover where it grows, together with the environmental and geographical conditions that favor its survival.

WHERE DOES AGAVE GROW?

Despite its reputation for favoring hot and dry climates, agave also grows in more humid environments. Do not allow a mythical search for the perfect piña to ruin a potentially fabulous experience! Remember that regardless of your location, the quality and characteristics of the finished mezcal in your bottle are not simply influenced by the species and growing conditions of the selected agave but also by secondary raw materials and distillation practices. In fact, many professional mezcaleros who acquired their knowledge from old-time mezcal-makers still choose to embellish venerable recipes to create new and intriguing mezcal varieties. Ultimately, the art of mezcal-making is imbued with pride in a job well done, and creativity is seldom far behind.

In the United States, agaves are found across the Southwest, from Utah to the Mexican border. About forty of the one hundred and fifty U.S. species grow in the Sonoran Desert. Most thrive in semi-arid habitats such as oak-pine woodlands and desert grasslands. They favor rocky, well-drained slopes. Their range extends southward through most of Mexico, where almost all of North American species occur.

Agaves are also found in Central and South America and the Caribbean, as well as in India and parts of sub-Saharan Africa. They are used for many purposes. Most species have extremely fibrous leaves. Their fibers have long been worked into an array of items, including brushes, nets, ropes, sandals, and sleeping mats. Agaves such as sisal, henequen, and cantala are most often relied upon for this purpose. Although native to Central America, these agave species are now cultivated in South America, parts of Africa, the Philippines, Taiwan, and Southeast Asia. Agave has other beneficial uses. For instance, the biofuels industry converts spent agave leaves that are discarded after distillation into alternative fuel while the sweet sap of some agave species is a welcome addition to many kitchens as a healthy natural sweetener.

Agaves bear long leathery or succulent leaves, which may reach 8 feet (2.5 meters) in length depending on the species (Petruzzello, 2023). The leaves form a rosette and, when they are removed, the plant's thick stem, or piña, is revealed. This is extremely rich in carbohydrates called inulin, which peak just before the plant flowers, making it an ideal choice for producing both mezcal and natural sweeteners. The raw sap is toxic, however, and stems must be cooked before consumption.

When it comes to mezcal, Mexico is traditionally its production stronghold. Several regions produce a range of mezcals with different flavor profiles. These include (The Producers: Geography, n.d.):

- In northwestern Mexico's Bacanora region, mezcals are mostly derived from wild *Agave pacifica* plants, which grow in the Sonora Mountains and are found nowhere else in the world. This creates a dry mezcal with complex flavors and an earthy aftertaste. Producers often add almonds or pine nuts early in the distillation process to augment these flavors.

- *Dasylirion wheeleri*, also known as the desert spoon, is native to northern Mexico, New Mexico, the Texas Hill Country, and western Texas. It is used to produce an agave spirit called sotol, which is the state drink of the Mexican states of Chihuahua, Durango, and Coahuila. Its production mimics that of the artisanal mezcals of Central Mexico.

- The true home of traditional mezcal is confined to the Mexican regions of Durango, Guanajuato, Guerrero, Michoacán, Oaxaca, Puebla, San Luis Potosi, Tamaulipas, and Zacatecas. These mezcals are all unique to the areas where they are produced and can be made from any local agave species. Their pleasant flavors (fruity or floral, herbal or earthy, peppery or spicy) are as varied as the agaves that gave them birth and the mezcaleros who nurtured them.

- Tequila has appellation of origin status, and the name can be used only for spirits produced in Jalisco and specific municipalities in Tamaulipas, Nayarit, Michoacán, and Guanajuato using Blue Weber agaves. The ones that thrive in the red volcanic soils of the Jalisco highlands confer sweet, floral, citrusy, and fruity flavors. Agaves cultivated in the lowlands impart bold peppery, earthy, herbal, and mineral-like flavors and aromas to the spirit.

- The Raicilla region centers on the Pacific coastal town of Puerto Vallarta in Jalisco. Its mezcals were legalized for export to the United States in 2014. Distilled from wild agaves such as chico agave and *Agave maximiliana*, they have tropical fruit flavors and tend to be sweet and robust.

AGAVE AND MEZCAL FLAVOR PROFILES

New mezcal drinkers want to know everything they can about the mezcals they drink. How were the spirits distilled and what materials were used? What agave species created the unique flavors they're sipping?

One of the agave species most commonly used for mezcal is *Agave espadin*, from which over 75% of certified mezcals were derived in 2014. The plant is tough and matures within eight years, which is relatively quick for agave. Most species mature within an average time of twelve to fifteen years, with some taking as long as thirty years (Rubenstein, 2015).

Demand is soaring for the mezcals derived from the wild agaves native to Oaxaca, like sweet tobalá and fiery cuishe, as well as barril, tepextate, arroqueño, and countless others. A big contributing factor to the flavors of mezcal is what winemakers in their vineyards refer to as the *terroir*, where taste is determined by the location and habitat of the plants—soil types, elevation of the land, regional ecosystems, and climate. Terroir's impact is perhaps as noteworthy in the realm of mezcal as it is in that of wine. It can contribute to flavors so distinctive that connoisseurs can distinguish between a spirit produced from local plants and one distilled from plants grown some distance away. Of course, villages and producers also apply individual production methods, further adding to mezcal's diversity and great worth in an age when the trend is toward homogeneity.

HOW AGAVE HANDLES ADVERSE WEATHER

Agave grows well in naturally arid regions such as the American Southwest, but can drought damage agave?

Research conducted in the 2010s indicated that agave can thrive in drought conditions due to the plant's unusual approach to photosynthesis, the means by which plants use light to synthesize sugars that they convert into energy to fuel growth, flowering, and reproduction (English, 2012).

In most green plants, this means that foliage takes in carbon dioxide and water vapor from the air and soil respectively. Inside plant cells, the water is transformed into oxygen and the carbon dioxide is used to form glucose. The oxygen is released back into the air and energy is stored within the glucose molecules. Light energy derived from sunshine is converted into chemical energy that the plant uses.

There is a beautiful symbiosis between plants, which rely on carbon dioxide to survive and emit oxygen, and animals which rely on oxygen to survive and exhale carbon dioxide.

Like many other plants that thrive in arid regions, agaves make use of a method known as crassulacean acid metabolism (CAM) to reduce water loss. With most plants, water is pulled up from the roots through the plant during the day. The excess is released through tiny pores in the leaves called *stomata*. However, CAM means that the plants close their stomata during the day, thus preventing water loss, and open them at night. Then, while the world sleeps, the open stomata draw in carbon dioxide, which they'll convert to energy the next day. Farmers and backyard growers should consider agave a very astute choice for a crop in desert areas.

Sub-freezing temperatures can adversely affect agave cultivation, especially if the cold lasts for several hours. In 2011, a sudden cold snap froze 60% of northern Mexico's mature agave plants. This was a rare tragedy. From times immemorial, farmers have dealt with weather-related trials. They have always kept their eye on the sky, but today they're ahead of the game. Weather apps on their cell phones warn them of impending danger long before it reaches their plot of land.

Modern farmers have other new defense systems in their arsenals. Biodegradable *anti-transpirant* sprays provide a nearly invisible seal around vulnerable leaves, which can reduce the risk of cold damage. Simply covering plants with a layer of plastic can afford several degrees of frost protection by trapping a layer of warmer air around the foliage.

A few plants are easy to cover, but a larger crop poses a greater logistical challenge. As in so many aspects of life, a challenge can present opportunity.

A personal friend of mine farmed cherries in California's Central Valley for decades. Every few years, an unseasonably late rain would destroy most of the region's cherry crop. Thin-skinned cherries poorly tolerate the osmotic pressure introduced by drops of water being absorbed into their sugary interiors, so after a rain event most cherries crack open within a couple of days.

In response, my friend trained his cherry trees onto a trellis system across which he could easily stretch plastic tarps in the Spring. When rain damaged his neighbors' cherry crops, the shrinking fruit supply would cause prices to skyrocket. My friend sold his protected and perfect cherries for a handsome premium, turning the area's loss into a personal boon.

As with cherries, untimely precipitation poses a challenge for agaves. Sustained rain can waterlog the desert soil and induce root rot. A raised bed and covering system can mitigate this risk, as well as provide protection from frost. Access to healthy agave after a cold snap could translate into a huge premium for your crop and special bragging rights for that year's mezcal. If you have an entrepreneurial or engineering bent, you might use your backyard agave planting as an outdoor laboratory in which to develop your own covering system. Who knows? This could be a valuable solution that farmers would be willing to buy, and your humble hobby could turn into a profitable commercial enterprise!

Don't let the vicissitudes of farming deter you from pursuing your dream! In Chapter 9, we will explore in-depth how you too can become an agave farmer, even in a modest backyard.

In response to rising demand, many Mexican mezcal producers grow their own agaves. Given how many years it takes for an agave plant to mature, producers are forecasting demand years in advance. Of course, this is also true of tree and vine crops. I once grew artichoke plants in my garden and had to wait seven years for the first harvest, so I have learned firsthand the importance of patience!

Turning back to Mexico, most commercial agave plantations are devoted to *Agave espadin*. To maintain the genetic diversity promoting healthy plants that are resilient and disease-resistant, buds are planted in the same fields where they originally grew, with some plants allowed to go to seed to ensure that they are not identical to their mothers. Indeed, farmers understand that excessive use of monoculture could bring about a decline in the wonderful diversity that is inherent in mezcal and remains a significant part of its charm and attraction.

In the next chapter we'll find out more about which varieties of agave are used for mezcal production, but before continuing, let's pause to enjoy a moment in the agave landscape.

Oh, give me land, lots of land under starry skies above
Don't fence me in
Let me ride through the wide open country that I love
Don't fence me in
Let me be by myself in the evenin' breeze
And listen to the murmur of the cottonwood trees
Send me off forever but I ask you please
Don't fence me in
Just turn me loose, let me straddle my old saddle
Underneath the western skies
On my Cayuse, let me wander over yonder
Till I see the mountains rise I want to ride to the ridge where the west commences
And gaze at the moon till I lose my senses
And I can't look at hobbles and I can't stand fences
Don't fence me in

- Bing Crosby, "Don't Fence Me In"

AGAVE VARIETIES AND THEIR UNIQUE FLAVORS

> *Deserts are very dry places, but plants can still grow there. Desert plants collect and use water in special ways.*
>
> — JULIE PENN

> *Night comes to the desert all at once, as if someone turned off the light.*
>
> — JOYCE CAROL OATES

Do you wonder what agaves are used to produce all the different types of mezcal available in Mexico and abroad? This chapter will explain how each agave variety contributes to the special flavor profile of a particular mezcal. You'll learn to appreciate the subtleties of the different agave species and understand their pivotal role in defining the quality and taste of the final spirit.

INTRODUCTION TO AGAVES

Around two hundred different species of succulent plants are considered agaves. In the Americas, these large, hardy plants are native to the southwestern United States and Mexico (Agave, n.d.). Oddly enough, they belong to the asparagus family, *Asparagaceae*, which also includes yuccas and hostas. In general, agaves are evergreen plants that bear thick, durable, fleshy leaves in a rosette formation. The leaves usually have spiny teeth along the edges and frequently terminate in a sharp, robust thorn.

When agaves flower, the sight is nothing short of spectacular. The plant sends up a towering flower spike, or *quiote*, that may be as tall as 15 feet (5 meters), topped with a colorful cluster of flowers (Agave, n.d.). Most agaves flower only once in their lives before dying. During their lifetimes, agaves produce numerous pups to compensate for the plant's ultimate demise. Mezcaleros remove the flower spike when it appears, encouraging the plant to raise the sugar levels of its sap rather than use energy for producing flowers and seeds.

AGAVE VARIETIES FOR MEZCAL

When it comes to choosing agave varieties for making your own mezcal, it's important to know that production methods determine the final outcome more than agave species. Two producers could use the same agave species but achieve very different results because of the way they process the ingredients.

Of the two hundred species of agave, around forty to fifty can readily be used to make mezcal. Each species may contain several similar, but not identical, varieties. To further complicate matters, many mezcaleros use names that are specific to their country, region, or specific area. The varieties listed below are most common in mezcal production (McKirdy, 2020):

Espadin (*Agave angustifolia*)

Espadin certainly deserves its reputation as the "workhorse" of the agave world; no other type even comes close. This most-used variety bears gray-green foliage with sharp teeth. It's less fibrous than other agaves. This means it is easier to crush it after roasting is completed. It also contains high amounts of a carbohydrate called inulin, which renders the conversion of plant sugars into alcohol more efficient. Espadin agaves mature faster than other species and can be harvested within eight years of planting. Mezcals made from espadin sometimes have a taste reminiscent of tequila. This is because the Blue Weber agave used in tequila production is a sub-species of *Agave angustifolia*. Espadin is widely used, but don't think of it as some sort of subpar generic. The spirits distilled from its heart and piña are far from boring; some of the most celebrated mezcals in the world are produced from this variety.

Tobalá (*Agave potatorum*)

This rare agave species is only found in southern Mexico's premier mezcal-producing regions: Guerrero, Michoacán, Oaxaca, and Puebla. Unlike many other agave types, this uncommon variety does not grow pups. It also uses bats and birds to spread its seeds. Tobalá plants take ten to fifteen years to mature and have limited sap and inulin content, which means that the mezcal produced from them is a very scarce drink. Flavors tend to be earthy and fruity. This is one of the pricier mezcals.

Cuishe, Bicuishe, Madre Cuishe, Barril, Mexicano, Tobaziche, Verde (Agave karwinskii)

These agave varieties grow in the states of Puebla and Oaxaca, with tobaziche being one of the best. *Agave karwinskii* is usually harvested from the wild and has a very singular appearance, with a thick elongated piña that takes around ten years to develop. Mezcals made with *Agave karwinskii* have herbal, mineral-like flavors and chalky textures.

Cuixe (Agave karwinskii var. covillei)

Grown in Oaxaca, this agave variety is rare and highly sought after. The mezcal it produces is known for its complex smoky and earthy flavors with hints of spices, tropical fruits, and subtle sweetness. This mezcal has a smooth, almost silky texture and can be consumed *neat*, as is, or added to cocktails.

Arroqueño (Agave americana)

Frequently referred to as the "American Century Plant", this stunning, statuesque agave has broad, blue-green leaves with slightly toothed edges. It grows to 10 feet (3 meters) wide. Think about its girth! When planted in parks and gardens or for cultivation, it needs plenty of space. Not only is *Agave americana* exceedingly rare, but it also needs a good twenty-five years to mature. Its mezcal flavors tend to be floral, slightly astringent, and fresh.

Pulquero, Rayo, Coyote, Sierra Negra, Serrudo, Teometl, Serrano, Blanco, De Castilla (Agave americana oaxacensis)

These gigantic *silvestre*, or wild, agaves constitute several varieties and grow naturally in Miahautian, Oaxaca, often reaching heights of around ten meters, or 32 feet (10 meters) (*Agave americana*). They are often harvested at the age of fourteen years, although some may take as long as thirty years to mature fully. These rare mezcals, with sweet, fruity flavors, are crafted according to traditional methods. To boost their commercial value, they are only produced in small batches. This deliberate restraint also helps conserve existing wild agaves while their replacements grow undisturbed. Additionally, a number of more vigorous projects focus on semi-cultivating the otherwise scarce plants, thus speeding up the process of replenishing wild stock.

Tepeztate or Tepextate (*Agave marmorata*)

Endemic to Guerrero and Oaxaca and still found nowhere else on earth, *Agave marmorata*, or marbled agave, is one of the slowest-growing agaves, taking twenty-five to thirty-five years to mature before sending up a magnificent flower spike topped with clusters of striking yellow flowers (Maguey tepeztate, n.d.). One of the most unusual and attractive agaves, this variety has strange, twisted leaves. It grows wild in dry, rocky soils among stones and boulders, and can survive very extreme conditions. Mezcal producers frequently harvest these plants when they are fifteen years old. The mezcal is made the traditional way using red oak and mesquite woods for roasting. Fermentation takes place in pine and oak vats that are open to the air. Sweet, fruity flavors are released during the double distillation process in copper stills.

Cenizo (*Agave durangensis*)

This is the agave most often used for mezcal-making in Durango, a state in northwestern Mexico. *Cenizo* also grows in the states of Michoacán, Puebla, and Jalisco. It is found at high altitudes (up to 8,500 feet) and thrives in dry, cold environments.

The flavor profiles of its mezcals are strongly influenced by the microclimate of the particular spots where the agaves were grown and harvested. Agaves sited in valleys differ from those grown on mountainsides, and plants maturing on a north-facing slope contrast significantly in character from their relatives flourishing on south-facing slopes. High altitude amplifies the biochemical effect of otherwise minor variations in plots of land.

Such distinctions make for a more exciting tasting experience. Despite the family differences, Cenizo usually opens with a warm floral or citric nose, sometimes with aspects of fresh cut aloe vera. There are notes of smoky barbeque or mesquite, and the finish is long and smooth with hints of chocolate, raisins, and woody bark.

Green Giant (Agave salmiana)

This wild agave variety thrives in the eastern part of San Luis Potosí, although the mezcal it creates is made some distance away in Zacatecas, which lies north of Oaxaca. The distillation process results in a mezcal that has a light and citric flavor. The Green Giant isn't just massive; it also yields a very herbaceous mezcal, not unlike a tincture of freshly cut grass. The flavor profile is sweet and slightly spicy, with notes of grapefruit, green chili, oregano, mint, and fennel.

Cupreata (Agave papalometl)

Cupreata is the name of not one, but several agave varieties that grow in different Mexican regions. Although this wild agave's appearance is rather reminiscent of tobalá, its botanical name resembles the word for "butterfly" in the Nahuatl language. Perhaps a yet undiscovered Spanish manuscript, centuries-old, records the Aztec epic tale or poetic musings that may have inspired the naming of this succulent. I like to envision a butterfly flitting from plant to plant and slowly journeying through various Mexican states where *Agave papalometl* grows. Cupreata from all regions deserves to be lauded for its delectable mezcals, known for usually earthy and smoky flavor profiles.

Lechuguilla (*Agave maximiliana*)

This sturdy mountain succulent was named after the ill-fated Austrian archduke who was for a few short years emperor of Mexico, and the memory of Emperor Maximilian's tragic destiny only gives depth to one of the many anecdotes that add color to larger historical events and otherwise commonplace surroundings. In 1865, while Maximilian I was emperor of Mexico, brothers Pedro and Ignacio Blasquez were scholarly mezcaleros who made pulque on their property in Puebla. After years of careful study, they composed about the *maguey* an eloquent treatise that they meant as an instructive scientific manual and a tribute to a plant that enriched their homeland with what they described as its many uses, including medical and industrial applications. Because of the fine quality of the Lechuguilla agave, the Brothers Blasquez dedicated it to their emperor. Its name, *Agave maximiliana* will forever enshrine this agave variety as a bookmark in a momentous chapter of Mexican history (Blasquez and Blasquez, 1865).

Maximilian's tragedy is a colorful and salient episode in the history of Mexico. A small Mexican delegation seeking a European royal to govern their land was encouraged by Napoleon III of France to select the Austrian royal because of his complicated pedigree. Maximilian may have had the right identity, but he did not have the expertise or the allies required to successfully administer the country. Napoleon III sent a small detachment of French soldiers to support Maximilian's claim to the throne of Mexico, but the new emperor's view of his role did not match what was needed to establish a durable power structure. He was accused of embarking on a philosophical liberal reverie instead of raising an army and establishing an effective government. He and the small contingent that protected him were soon overcome by the army of Benito Juárez, who would go on to become the President of Mexico. Today, Mexico celebrates the defeat of Maximilian on Cinco de Mayo, a national holiday.

Lechuguilla has found its way into Mexican history, but this graceful plant can stand on its own for its loveliness. It can do double duty as a beautiful ornamental and a source for mezcal production. Distilled in the small town of Mascota in Jalisco, this raicilla mezcal is made according to traditional methods. The agaves are roasted in adobe ovens above ground rather than in pits. The charred agave is scraped off after roasting, reducing the smokiness of the mezcal and giving it earthy, herbal flavors.

Sotol (Dasylirion wheeleri)

Originally from the Chihuahua Desert that extends from northern Mexico to the southwestern United States, this plant results in a spirit that has strong mineral and earthy flavors and aromas, with notes of stone fruit, mint, and caramel. It is said that Sotol is technically not a mezcal, but its close cousin. One happy characteristic of the shrub is that after its piñas are harvested, it can easily regrow plants from the roots. Mexico controls the production of its Sotol and requires permits to harvest wild plants. The drink is increasingly prized, but each drop counts. Only one bottle of mezcal can be distilled from each piña (Stephens, 2023).

FLAVOR PROFILES OF MEZCAL VARIETIES

In the first chapter, we defined the indispensable term *terroir* and explained its importance for both the wine and mezcal industries. Terroir, however, is but one piece of the puzzle. We have just reviewed a number of major agave varieties that have become enshrined in the go-to list of perfect raw piñas. Whether you are just beginning to learn about mezcal, want to impress your date at some future tasting, or think about tackling an intimidating new hobby, remember that production factors such as distillation, storage, and aging methods play a big role in the final results.

Aging mezcal definitely influences its aroma, flavor, and quality. When mezcal is aged in oak barrels, its flavors become more complex and diverse. Young mezcals tend to have fresher, cleaner flavors, whereas aged ones are more intriguing. How the agave piñas are roasted and whether distillation is done in clay pots or copper or columnar stills affects the final outcome. Mezcaleros are like winemakers. They get to make decisions on how the end product will taste, and why. Some focus on tradition and attempt to perpetuate ancient ways, while others opt for more modern methods in their commercial production. All these factors, with their diverse challenges and advantages, strongly contribute to the final flavor of the mezcal.

Common Mezcal Flavor Profiles

After reviewing the many factors that were in play to create the drink in your special bottle, you may wonder if it is possible to make generalizations about flavor profiles. However, just as it is with wine, it is not just feasible but part of the fun. Some of the more common mezcal flavor profiles are listed below (Eastman, n.d.):

- Most mezcals are smoky and earthy with a trace of sweetness. The majority of mezcals with this profile are produced from espadin agaves.
- Fruity, sweet mezcals often include notes of banana, pineapple, or tropical fruit and are commonly derived from tobalá or tepeztate agave varieties.
- Peppery, spicy flavors with hints of cinnamon, nutmeg, and black pepper often characterize mezcals made from espadin, tobalá, and tepeztate agaves.
- Mezcals created using tobalá or cuixe agave varieties can also have herbal or floral flavor profiles, including mint, basil, jasmine, or rose.
- Nutty, woody flavor profiles with a touch of almond, cedar, or hazelnut are characteristic of many mezcals distilled from coyote or tepeztate agave varieties.

Agave Forward Flavors

The term *agave forward* describes a mezcal produced with a focus on the flavors and aromas naturally released by a specific variety of agave rather than on the secondary ingredients or flavors that are coaxed into it by the mezcalero. The idea is to focus on the sweetness, fruitiness, or earthiness produced by the agave during roasting, fermentation, and distillation without adding spices, smoke, or other flavors which could overwhelm these delicate taste sensations. The only drawback is that results, however excellent, are inconsistent with this method of production, as the slight differences between plants cannot be mitigated.

Environmental Factors

Within agave-growing regions, environmental variations help deliver different flavor profiles. Wild, uncultivated agaves result in extremely diverse flavors that were determined in part by the mysterious or storied wilderness where they grew. The resulting mezcals range from spicy and smoky to earthy and herbaceous.

The agaves used for highland or plateau (*altiplano*) mezcals grow in the cool and dry weather of Mexico's high plateaus. This results in clear floral or fruity flavor profiles, often with notes of green apple, citrus, and herbaceous plants.

As you would expect, lowland or hot land (*tierra caliente*) mezcals are produced from agaves that flourish in warm, humid, and tropical conditions, resulting in sweeter, full-bodied flavors reminiscent of ripe fruit, honey, and caramel. When agaves grow near the coast, the mezcals they create will have briny, smoky flavors with hints of seaweed, iodine, and sea salt.

APPRECIATING MEZCAL'S FLAVOR NUANCES

The maturation of the succulent and the processes that convert its sap into mezcal bring out the secret flavors of the agave that grew massively in bright sunshine beneath the skies of Mexico or America's Southwest. Savoring the complex tastes and aromas of the drink in front of you should be done in an unhurried and appreciative manner. Although it may be a great strategy to establish dominance at a double date, hurling your drink back like a shot is not the way to get the most out of your mezcal-tasting. As most mezcals are around 45% alcohol by volume (*ABV*) (or 90 proof), it's advisable to sip them extremely slowly anyway (Newman, 2023). This will enable you to fully appraise and relish the full range of their incredible, complex flavors. The first sip will probably taste quite different from the last as your palate opens up. Avoid adding ice—it would dilute the drink's unique gustatory palette. Mezcal is usually consumed neat at room temperature, so its flavors can develop fully.

You can sip your mezcal from a small wine glass or champagne flute, as shot glasses often concentrate the aromas once the alcohol evaporates. However, the professionals suggest that it's best to drink it from a *copita*, in this case a wide-mouthed clay vessel that infuses the flavors and aromas as you sip. This is bound to impress your date!

Set the scene of your tasting to enhance the experience. Find a comfortable spot in the sunshine or shade, by a crackling fireplace, or with some appreciative friends.

Before sipping, take a moment to enjoy the unique aromas of the mezcal. Dab a small amount on the back of your hand or wrist and rub it into your skin. This will help you to savor the special aromas of any particular mezcal. Once the alcohol evaporates, you'll be left with the scents of the compounds released during the roasting of the agave. This will awaken your curiosity.

Finally, sip. Begin slowly, allowing the flavor to gently open up your palate. Then, take another very small sip and leave the spirit on your tongue for a few seconds to stimulate your taste buds. The flavors will be complex—the agave developed them over many years, after all. Allow your taste buds to experience every nuance of taste and flavor. As you become an old-hand at mezcal tasting, you will learn to identify each unique flavor. When you sip a new mezcal, you will find you can embrace its complexity.

In the next chapter, you'll find out how Mexicans fashion their fiery, unique mezcals from the hearts of hardy, drought-resistant plants that do not make you think of a drink when you first encounter them.

Los seis días a paso largo en el desierto
Las estrellas nos guiaban y daban tiempo Los coyotes, las arañas y
serpientes
Desafiándonos para ver si éramos fuertes Hay que ser muy valiente para
dejar su tierra, paisano!

Those six days of long strides in the desert
The stars guiding us and giving us time
The coyotes, the spiders and snakes Challenging us to see if we were
strong
You must be very brave to leave your country, countryman!

- Banda Yurirense, "El Desierto"

FROM AGAVE TO MEZCAL: THE OAXACAN METHOD

> *The production of heat alone is not sufficient to give birth to impelling power: It is necessary that there should also be cold; without it, the heat would be useless.*

> — SADI CARNOT

> *When the heat is on, make sure you're not that first pancake.*

> — WYATT B. PRINGLE, JR.

In this chapter, you'll discover the intricate, traditional methods Mexican mezcaleros use to make mezcal. This will serve to inspire and inform your own mezcal-making efforts.

TRADITIONAL OAXACAN MEZCAL PRODUCTION

Traditional mezcal production involves five or six steps, each of which is infused with a mezcalero's particular goals and traditions. The process begins with the long-term cultivation of agave plants when they are not harvested from the wild. The production of mezcal involves (Alex, 2023):

1. Harvesting
2. Roasting
3. Crushing or milling
4. Fermenting
5. Distilling
6. Aging (optional)

Harvesting Agave

On agave plantations, the person responsible for harvesting the agave piñas is known as a *jimador*. These artisans are greatly respected in Mexico, where their skills are traditionally passed down through generations. Jimadors decide when agaves are ready for harvesting, as each plant grows and matures at its own rate. Today, many producers also use scientific testing to determine the ideal harvesting time based on the sugar content of the plant's sap —a measurement known as Brix. Winegrape growers also rely on Brix measurements for similar purposes. For tequila, the sugar content has to be at least 24% (24 Brix) by law, but some producers harvest plants with a much higher sugar content. Plants grown in the highlands tend to have more sugars than those grown at lower elevations. The higher the sugar content, the higher the alcohol content of the final spirits will be (Chadwick, 2007). Plant sugars in mature plants peak at the end of the dry season, as rain dilutes the sugars in the sap.

Once the agave is fully mature, its flower stalk begins to grow. The jimador cuts it down, thereby encouraging the plant to develop the piña, which will be harvested two to three months later (Tequila.net, n.d.). This needs to be done quickly, as the flower stalk is fully developed within a week of its first appearance (Chadwick, 2007). The piña should be harvested when the sugar content of the sap is at its highest but before it ferments. Other indications of ripeness are when the piña shrinks slightly and develops a maroon tint. Red spots will appear on plant leaves, and they may turn darker with wrinkled tips or become yellow-green near the base. The remnant of the flower stalk also starts developing shoots.

By this time, the average agave will have grown around 200 leaves, and it is the jimador's job to cut them off to expose the piña. This is done in less than a minute with a long-handled tool called a *coa*. Only when the leaves are removed is it possible to see the size of the piña, as it varies considerably from plant to plant and cannot be ascertained from the stature of the succulent. Once almost all leaves are gone, the jimador severs the piña from the root system and lops off the remainder of the leaves. Most jimadors trim a large agave within less than six minutes and can harvest a ton of piñas each day (Chadwick, 2007). The trimmed piñas are placed on trucks for transport. Donkeys are sometimes used to move the piñas from the fields to the waiting trucks. Once they reach the distillery, or *palenque*, they are cut into halves or quarters.

Roasting

Plants store energy in the form of starches to improve disease resistance. In agaves, the starches reside in a substance known as inulin. Roasting agave piñas converts the inulin into glucose and fructose, simple sugars that transform into alcohol during fermentation. The amount of sugar present in the piñas after roasting also affects the rate and efficacy of fermentation. Sometimes different agave varieties are blended during roasting, creating novel and often adventurous combinations.

After harvesting, the piñas are transported to the *palenque*, which has a deep earthen pit. This pit is filled with wood from local trees and set alight. The fire is encircled with a layer of rocks and left to burn for about five to six hours until it has reduced to hot coals (Wally, 2022). This ensures that the heat is evenly distributed. The fire probably won't get hotter than it is now. Everything is then covered with a layer of *bagasse*, the material left over after the piñas have been crushed and their juice extracted. Some producers use palm branches for this purpose if they are available locally. This insulates the piñas from the hot rocks. The piñas are layered on the rocks according to size, with the larger ones at the bottom and the smaller ones on top. The mound is carefully constructed to ensure that they roast evenly.

After this, the piñas are covered first with agave leaves and then with a layer of straw mats, grain sacks, and sand in the shape of a volcano. Some producers use a wet canvas tarp, which is then covered with the sand. A small opening is left at the top of the mound, and the mezcalero pours fresh water into it to release the smoke trapped inside. The piñas are left to roast for around two to three days while the heat converts the carbohydrates into sugars (Lewis, n.d.). This roasting process is what gives mezcals their smoky flavors.

Roasting might sound easy, but it's a surprisingly fine art. If you get it wrong and the piñas scorch and burn, the batch may be ruined. Given the length of time it takes for agave to grow and the potential value of your mezcal, the roasting process must be handled with care.

Such an elementary mistake is akin to using the wrong yeast to make wine. Years ago, I participated in a doomed effort to make a small batch of wine. None of the contenders had ever before attempted the feat. All went reasonably well until fermentation came to a screeching halt. After running for reinforcements, we discovered to our dismay that we had selected the wrong yeast, one that could not handle the exigencies of the high-sugar content of the grapes we had harvested. Fortunately, we learned that a new yeast could perhaps restart the process. We eventually chalked the episode up to lessons learned and tuition paid.

All in all, the time and effort devoted to study and preparation always pay off.

Milling

When the pit is uncovered, the piñas, which are toasty on the outside, are usually left in place to cool. If you break off a piece, it will taste sweet; people sometimes eat them like candy. The taste has been likened to a combination of grilled corn and lightly singed tropical fruit, with something of Oaxaca's desert breezes mixed in. At some factories, the charred piñas are removed from the pit once they've cooled and left to rest for about a month (Wally, 2022). They will often turn moldy during this time. No one worries about this too much—these molds also impart unique flavors to the mezcal.

Other producers don't do this but move on to the next phase of the process as soon as the piñas have cooled and been removed from the pit. The larger agave pieces are cut into smaller, hand-sized chunks with machetes and axes, as this is the ideal size for milling. The pieces are then transferred to a stone or wooden pit, although some distillers still use traditional, hollow logs. Sometimes, the roasted agave pieces are crushed laboriously by hand, using gigantic wooden mallets. As you can imagine, this ancient process takes quite a long time. Three men working for fourteen hours are only able to crush enough to fill one fermentation vat—but it's still done in places like Potrero and Bramaderos (Lewis, n.d.). Try to discover everything you can about the mezcal you're about to sample, including how it was made. Share the stories you are learning, and take time to honor those who worked hard to bring this spirit to you.

In more places, another traditional but slightly less labor-intensive method is used—employing a *tahona*, or Egyptian mill. This is a large circular stone that looks similar to a millstone with a hole in the middle. It is wheeled around a circular pit by a donkey or horse. Making mezcal is a family affair, and children are often enlisted to encourage the animals to pull the tahona around the pit. This pulverizes the agave pieces into a mash of roasted pulp and nectar called *mosto*. Although low-tech, the process is extremely effective.

The mosto is then transferred to wooden vats, or *tinas*. The dry, fibrous leftovers—the bagasse or *bagaso*—represent about 40% of the total weight of the harvested agave (Francisco, 2012). Bagasse is a recyclable product. It is collected and used for fuel or mulch, to make adobe, or to insulate the next batch of roasting piñas.

Fermentation

Fermentation is when the magic happens. Miniscule yeast cells eat the carbohydrates and sugars in the mosto, ultimately converting the sugars into alcohol. The crushed piñas and their juices are loaded into vats made from a variety of woods, including acacia, oak, cypress, or pine. Because wood is slightly porous, these have a minor influence on the final flavors of the mezcal. Most vats used for artisanal mezcal have a capacity of around 158.5–264 gallons (600–1,000 liters) (Terrazas, 2015).

Other Mezcal Vat Options

Besides wooden vats, other traditional containers may be chosen for mezcal-making. Ceramic pots, which have been in use for centuries, enable the creation of complex mezcals but have limited capacity, do not maintain temperature well, and break easily. In some regions, especially where ambient temperatures are high, fermentation pits are dug into the bedrock and lined with earth. On some farms, a large cowhide is hung over a wooden frame and the mosto is fermented under it.

A modern option is to employ stainless steel vats. This is a selection that is often made in larger factories. However, stainless steel vats are not porous and do not create the same complexity of flavors as wood or other traditional options.

Today, plastic is everywhere, and its use has even permeated the world of mezcal-making. It is durable, lightweight, and relatively easy to come by, as large plastic containers are used for water storage in many parts of Mexico and are supplied by the government. Like stainless steel, plastic can't imbue flavors in the same way as wood or clay, and there's also the risk that undesirable chemicals could leach from the plastic container into the fermenting mezcal.

Fermentation: Wet or Dry?

Wheelbarrows and pitchforks transfer the more fibrous material to the vat, while the nectar is collected in buckets and poured in. During fermentation, the mixture will bubble and expand significantly, so many producers only fill their vats halfway to allow for this (Terrazas, 2015). *Dry Fermentation* is the term used when only the pulp and its juices are fermented.

Mezcaleros monitor the alcoholic smell coming off the vat. When it becomes so strong as to be almost unbearable, they may decide to add water from local sources, including streams, rivers, and wells, to the mosto. The minerals in the water contribute to the final flavor of the mezcal. This is known as *Wet Fermentation*, and mezcaleros often use a mix of both in different vats.

The liquid interacts with wild yeasts that are naturally present in the surrounding environment, and fermentation begins. Most mezcal producers simply rely on these yeasts rather than adding cultured commercial ones, as almost all winemakers and tequila producers do. Using wild yeasts means that the results are harder to predict, but that's all part of the mystery of mezcal. Some producers even collect wild yeasts from a good batch, save them, and add them to the next fermentation.

A good fermentation looks a little like a dark, rich fruit cake, which bubbles as the yeasts do their work and the sugars break down. It is usually allowed to ferment for anything from three days to two weeks, depending on the types of agave, elevation, season, and ambient temperature (Terrazas, 2015). Fermentation happens faster during warmer weather and more slowly in cooler temperatures. In traditional mezcal-making, temperatures are monitored by making a hole in the agave mixture and inserting a tree branch or bamboo pole into the vat until it reaches the bottom. The tree limb is then pulled out and the temperature of the fermentation is estimated from the heat emanating from it.

The mixture bubbles furiously as the yeasts become active. A crust will often form on top of the ferment, and this needs to be removed to prevent the mosto from becoming unduly acidic. While some producers leave the crust on the mezcal, breaking it up enables more oxygen to enter the mosto, ultimately resulting in a richer, mellower spirit. The mezcalero constantly monitors the mosto's sugar levels, using a hollow log with instruments attached to get to the bottom of the vat.

Eventually, the bubbling stops, and a brown, sugary crust appears on the top of the vat. At this point, the mixture will often look and smell like apple cider vinegar. Once the mixture's alcohol content reaches 4%–9% ABV, with a sugar concentration of 0.4%, it is ready to be distilled (Terrazas, 2016).

Distillation

Distillation effectively concentrates the alcohols in the fermented mixture by evaporating them using heat and pressure. The idea is to separate the alcohol from the water, so the alcohol is retained while the water evaporates out. It then recondenses into liquid.

In most artisanal distilleries the stills used to be made from clay, but such stills have largely been replaced by small copper pot ones; the choice is usually reflected on bottle labels. Stills usually rest on a masonry base—rock, clay, and sometimes brick—that has a wood-fired oven underneath it. The ovens are often equipped with vent pipes.

To start the distillation process, the fermented liquid is transferred from the vats and poured into the still, usually by hand using 5-gallon (20-liter) buckets. Ladders are used to reach the bottoms of the vats. The solids are removed from the distillery by wheelbarrow. When the still is full of liquid and fibers, it is closed and the pot is connected to the condensing coil tank. To make tequila the fibers are removed entirely, but mezcaleros often select to leave them in during distillation, as they will impart more flavors to the spirit. This is akin to winemakers' allowing fermenting juice to absorb complex notes from grape skins and seeds. For mezcal makers, tending the fire during distillation is essential, as the temperature needs to be kept constant.

The results of the first distillation are extremely potent, at around 70% ABV. Traditional mezcal is usually distilled two to three times (Wally, 2022). During the second distillation, the mezcalero may add different esculents to put his stamp on the mezcal and contribute to its unique flavor. This can be anything from toasted corn to a handful of chilies or even a chicken breast. After the second—or third—distillation, when the acidity, methanol, and aldehyde levels are within the parameters prescribed by the Consejo Regulador, which regulates Mexican mezcal production, then the mezcal is ready for bottling. Very often, the mezcal needs to be diluted with water after the final distillation to reduce its alcohol content to around 40% ABV. Some traditional mezcals are bottled at full strength to maintain the flavor of the agave (Falkowitz, 2023).

AGING MEZCAL

Many mezcals are bottled and consumed without aging and in some areas, mezcaleros believe that the best spirits are never aged in wooden barrels. However in other Mexican villages, there are equally long-standing traditions of aging mezcal in barrels. Because competition in idea generation and product delivery usually benefits the consumer, mezcal aficionados can look forward to years of discovery and enjoyment.

The decision to store spirits in wood was made a long time ago. Cognac, whisky, and American bourbon are prime examples of spirits subject to this practice.

In the 1800s, storing spirits in wood was found to significantly alter its flavors. This may have been partly due to the practice of charring barrel interiors with fire. The cognac exported by the French to settlers in New Orleans was stored in charred barrels, which may have brought the practice to the western hemisphere. The effect of charring is well-appreciated among spirit connoisseurs to this day.

It's also possible that early *coopers* chose to torch the insides of their barrels to neutralize putrid residues of fish, poultry, or other perishable products previously stored therein.

In any case, the interaction of alcohol with wood (charred or not) stimulates the release of trace aromatic compounds that modify its flavor as it ages.

While records of intentionally aged mezcal usually go back to the 1920s, evidence exists that the spirit was being stored in barrels before the late 1800s (Bank, 2022). Unlike other distillers, mezcaleros experimenting with wood-aged mezcal didn't write down or publicize their findings. There is much about mezcal that is shrouded in mystery. As with other parts of our inheritance from distant forebears, surviving oral histories and songs, archaeological finds, property lines, place names, deeds and decrees, ship manifests, oblique references in personal letters and manuscripts, esoteric customs, even modern recipe secrets or family stories, all lead to fascinating trails for the history detective. No matter the exact timing, mezcal eventually found itself aging in wood and today's aficionados can enjoy both its improved, sophisticated, complex moods and the intellectual challenge and emotional wonder of a record that is still steeped in mystery.

Indeed over the last century, mezcaleros have found ways to use aging in oak barrels to impart additional subtleties and complexities of flavor to their mezcals. According to Mexican government regulations, joven mezcals are not aged in wood. Some producers label their bottles "madurado en vidrio", which means that the mezcal has been aged in glass for at least a year. In case you're wondering, this is possible, and it does significantly change the flavor (Bank, 2022). As mentioned previously, some additional categories of aged mezcals are known as reposado and añejo, together with extra añejo.

When aged in wood, mezcals turn straw-colored, gold, amber, or even brownish. The flavonoids present in the distillate confer desirable flavors, such as spices, coconut, and vanilla. Toasting the barrel tends to eliminate unwanted sulfur compounds and tart flavors. Many brands use recycled barrels previously used to produce and age other alcoholic beverages, such as wine, port, sherry, and whisky, to confer a pleasing range of flavors to their products and further differentiate their brands. Ensuring that the properties of the wood do not overwhelm the natural, complex flavors delivered by the agave is an art in itself. Maturation can enhance the natural flavors of the mezcal without overpowering them.

For a hobbyist, making mezcal obviously requires planning and basic equipment, but what is most needed is enthusiasm. At a time when more and more people live virtual and remote lives, mezcal-making can bring people together in a manner that echoes thousands of years of meaningful human undertakings. You need not have mezcalero genes in your DNA to launch your new endeavor. The process of roasting, milling, fermenting, and distilling, even the planting of agave, is best done with family and friends, in a festive atmosphere. As for your helpers, they will keep an eye on the calendar and be ready to bring the food when the big day arrives and you gather excitedly to sample your homemade fiery spirit with its own unique twist. Perhaps slices of oranges sprinkled with *sal de gusano* or worm salt can add adventure and authenticity to your celebration.

In the next chapter, you'll find out more about other agave-based drinks like tequila and pulque and how they compare to mezcal.

AN OVERVIEW OF AGAVE SPIRITS

Fermentation may have been a better invention than fire.

— DAVID WALLACE

Aging is supposed to be like a picture frame and, in this case, the picture is agave. You don't want the frame to overtake the picture but to bring out the best attributes and highlight them.

— CARLOS CAMARENA

By the time you've finished reading this chapter, you'll know more about agave spirits, their differences, and legal issues concerning names and labels.

DISTINGUISHING MEZCAL, TEQUILA, AND PULQUE

	Mezcal	Tequila	Pulque
Production Areas	Mexico: Mainly Oaxaca but also Durango, Guanajuato, Guerrero, Michoacán, Puebla, San Luis Potosí, Tamaulipas, and Zacatecas May not be called mezcal if produced elsewhere	Mexico: Jalisco and parts of Tamaulipas, Nayarit, Michoacán, Guanajuato May not be called tequila if produced elsewhere	Mexico: Estado de México, Hidalgo, Tlaxcala, Puebla No restrictions on production areas or use of name
Agaves Used	Made from over 30 different agave varieties	Blue Weber (azul) agave (minimum 51%)	Agave species similar to those used for mezcal
Alcohol Content	At least 40% ABV	40%–60% ABV	2%–7% ABV
Process	Piñas are roasted in pits lined with rocks and filled with charcoal to extract plant sugars. This results in pronounced smoky flavors. After this, the agave and nectar are milled, fermented, and distilled 2–3 times.	Piñas are cooked in an autoclave (steam pressure cooker) and steam-baked to release plant sugars. Cooked piñas are mixed with water and crushed to create a mash, which is fermented with added yeast. The resulting liquid is distilled twice.	The mature agave piña is opened up until the sweet sap (*aguamiel*, or honey water) flows out. Using an *acocote*, a long, hollow gourd with a hole at either end, the sap is collected. The initial yield is 0.2–5 gallons (1–18 liters), and it can continue producing for several months if the plant is properly tended. The sap is fermented in an open-air wooden container using natural, wild yeasts.

Aging Categories	Joven Reposado Añejo Madurado en vidrio (matured in glass)	Blanco Joven Reposado Añejo Extra Añejo	Not usually aged and highly perishable
Flavors	Many different and complex flavors—roasting confers a distinctive smokiness	Earthy, semi-sweet, agave flavor Tequila from the highlands tends to be fresher and greener. Tequila from the lowlands is fruitier and earthier.	Many different flavor profiles—may be sweet, light, and slightly fizzy to thick and creamy, bright and acidic to sweet
Worms	May include worms (larvae of moths that live on agave plants)	Never contains worms	Never contains worms
How to Drink	Usually sipped neat at room temperature	Shots Blanco is used to make margaritas and other cocktails. Aged tequilas may be drunk on the rocks or neat.	A popular drink that's often served with snacks, pulque may be blended with tropical fruits and other additives.

OTHER AGAVE SPIRITS

There is a growing demand for agave spirits, driven by a surge of interest in the U.S. market, although other parts of the world are also showing an interest. The most popular ones hailing from Mexico include bacanora, raicilla, and sotol. In 2022, sales of these spirits increased by 40% in the United States, and it is anticipated that the market will continue growing (Cawood, 2023).

Bacanora

This type of mezcal still relies on ancient production methods. Crafted primarily in northern Mexico's Sonora province and almost exclusively from *Agave pacifica*, bacanora is made much like other mezcals but is distilled only once (or occasionally twice).

In 1915, General Plutarco Elías Calles, the Governor of Sonora, imposed a statewide prohibition on alcohol production and consumption. Bacanora was the second most economically important product in Sonora at the time, so the ban devastated the livelihoods of farmers and producers. If caught, violators of the Governor's edict faced death by hanging, so agave plantations went fallow overnight (Goldberg, 2015). The ban was finally lifted in 1992, to the great relief of mezcal aficionados!

Bacanora has a smooth, mild flavor vaguely reminiscent of green apples and grass (Cawood, 2023).

Raicilla

This earthy, funky-tasting spirit has been produced in the western part of Jalisco—and one Nayarit municipality—for hundreds of years. Today, it may only be produced in these areas. It was first exported to the United States in 2014 (Cawood, 2023). Coastal raicilla is produced from *Agave angustifolia* and *Agave rhodacantha* using earthen pits and wood-fired stills. In the highlands, producers harvest wild *Agave maximiliana* and *Agave inaequidens* and use above-ground ovens and copper stills. Similar to regular mezcal, raicilla is made with juice extracted from the plants' piñas. Production methods vary, as different brands favor tried-and-true or innovative techniques to achieve their particular characteristics. However, raicilla lacks the smokiness of most mezcals and is more aromatic than tequila. Fans say it has hints of tropical fruit, citrus, peppers, wet earth, and minerals. In tropical Jalisco, raicilla is often served chilled, although in more temperate climates a room-temperature tasting allows for a more complete reveal of the spirit's subtle flavors.

Sotol

Although sotol is not made from agave but from a shrub called the desert spoon (*Dasylirion wheeleri*), it is considered an honorary mezcal because it's made using the same process. The desert spoon flourishes in desert climates from Oaxaca to Arizona and takes six to nine years to mature. It is an easy plant to grow as it requires little care. It also handles drought conditions without difficulty and is not normally prone to disease. And although it does especially well in sunny, hot, and dry deserts, it can thrive equally well in fairly humid conditions, as long as it is planted in a well-draining soil. After harvesting, hearts are usually roasted in above-ground—and occasionally underground—clay ovens before they are crushed, fermented, and distilled. The desert's dramatic temperature changes give the distilled spirit an earthy, mineral taste. Aging sotol in oak imparts additional flavors such as chocolate, vanilla, and charred wood. Since 2004, Mexican law has dictated that sotol production be limited to three Mexican states: Chihuahua, Coahuila, and Durango. However, these restrictions do not apply to the United States, so U.S. producers in areas where the desert spoon grows can make their own versions of this unusual, mezcal-like spirit (Morgan, 2023).

LEGALITIES AND LABELING

The words *mezcal* and *tequila* are now legally protected, and only certain Mexican states where they are produced are allowed to use these names on their bottles and labels. This is because these spirits have received a *denomination of origin* (DO). This is similar to a trademark and is owned by the state—Mexico in this case. It was registered by the World Intellectual Property Organization in Switzerland on March 9, 1995 (Francisco et al., 2012).

A denomination of origin:

- certifies the name of a region, place, or country where an agricultural or food product is produced.
- confirms that it originated there.
- confirms the product's quality or characteristics that are

enabled by the geographical environment where it grows or is produced.

- assures that the production, processing, and preparation of the product takes place in that specific geographical area.

In Mexico, the regulatory body for mezcal production is the Mexican Mezcal Regulatory Council (COMERCAM), which:

- manages a registry of agave plantations.
- certifies production factories and batches of mezcal produced for sale in Mexico and abroad.
- monitors the specifications of the official standard, or NOM.
- stipulates health and safety measures to be taken in factories and distilleries.
- sets out quality control procedures.
- stipulates labeling requirements (Francisco et al., 2012).

Only products that meet the COMERCAM requirements can carry this designation. DOs have the potential to create a sustainable manufacturing culture, ensuring quality, economic benefits, and environmental protection. They are also marketing tools for producers.

Mexico's *Secretaría de Economía* (Secretariat of Economy) believes that a product must first prove its worth by being used and consumed. After it has become popular with the public, it becomes eligible for protection by a DO or a similar declaration. Between 1994 and 2015, all states producing mezcal received this designation. If mezcal is not produced in the region authorized by the DO, it cannot be called mezcal and should be referred to as an agave spirit. Additionally, any spirit calling itself mezcal has to be produced entirely from agave. According to Mexican officials, the mezcal DO is the largest in the world, covering over 193 square miles (500 square kilometers) (Janzen, 2022).

In August 2016, the NOM approved the inclusion of aged mezcals in their standards. It stipulated aging times and promulgated regulations pertaining to the safety of the final product for consumption (Francisco et al., 2012).

In 2018, more Mexican states requested permission to be included in the DO, but mezcaleros in existing DO states successfully appealed through the courts to prevent this (Janzen, 2022). The mezcaleros claimed they wished to avoid having their traditional locations, defined by hundreds of years of artisanal production, quashed by alien and sometimes large operations that were strangers to the culture and the art of the craft. The states wanting to be included lodged their own appeals. The cases have yet to be resolved.

Some argue that the word *mezcal* is a generic term for many agave distillates produced across Mexico and it would have been more accurate to regionalize the designation, for example, referring to a spirit as being "Mezcal de Oaxaca" or "Mezcal de Guerrero". An added challenge is that opening the DO to other Mexican states could lead mezcal from foreign countries to be designated to those countries, in which case mezcal would effectively no longer be tied to its Mexican roots.

The size of the DO notwithstanding, consumers benefit when large companies using state-of-the-art technology compete side by side with small mom-and-pop ventures that preserve and perfect ancient tools and techniques steeped in deeply meaningful traditions. Customers can choose whether to purchase highly consistent products from more impersonal sources or do business with artisanal producers whose small-batch and highly distinctive spirits tell a story that is unique to each brand and even to each bottle.

DO Tequila

Tequila production has risen over time, due in part to growing interest in Jalisco's capital, Guadalajara. The port of Puerto Vallarta also facilitates export. On large-scale, privately-owned farms or *haciendas*, separate labor teams efficiently harvest and process agaves. This makes it easier to scale up production to meet rising demand. In regions such as Oaxaca and Guerrero, where land ownership has historically been focused on smallholdings, the distilling culture developed very differently. The question in Jalisco was not whether tequila would enter the international market, but when.

The DO tequila standard was adopted as far back as 1974 (Mezcaleria, n.d.). The government's effort to secure the livelihood of tequila makers had some unintended consequences. Small-scale producers, along with their time-honored traditional production methods, were sacrificed in favor of large enterprises, as the latter could more effectively meet the new regulations. Product diversity also suffered, thus further harming small businesses and reducing consumer choices. The designation specified that *Agave tequilana weber* (Blue Weber agave) had to be the dominant ingredient, although other agaves had previously been used. Several tequila distillations where these other agaves had been used became *mixtos*. In addition, 49% of the sugars used could be of unknown origin (Mezcaleria, n.d.). There has recently been a revival of old techniques and an attempt at greater diversity, mainly by small family-run operations wishing to carve a niche for themselves in the midst of giant, protected brands.

DO Mezcal

Introduced in 1994, the DO mezcal in many ways emulated the DO tequila. Again, it left out small operations that had long maintained unique mezcal-making or ancestral traditions precisely because of the lack of government intervention (Vasquez, 2021). Besides prescribing the region of origin, the standard did not acknowledge traditional methods of production. For example, it stipulated barrel aging (little mezcal is aged in barrels) and allowed the addition of foreign sugars during fermentation, which is usually avoided by traditional producers. As a result, many distillers are now sacrificing time-honored production methods to secure the desirable DO mezcal label. Sadly, this comes at the expense of product diversity and flavor. It is ironic that government efforts intended to protect historic mezcal traditions in authentic mezcal locations may cause the loss of ancient skills and the weakening of local appellations.

Several producers actually saw their mezcals banned after the state classified them as inferior, only to later retract this and implement regulations mandating production methods that would compromise the uniqueness of Mexican mezcal. Many landowners and producers are therefore opposed to the DO.

In 2017, the DO was amended to create three categories of mezcal (Vasquez, 2021). Having three groups allows for barrel aging and the introduction of agave worms.

The DO mandates that mezcal be created entirely from agave, but its standards do not specify the use of colorings, flavorings, or any additives added during processing or to the final product. Several mezcaleros see this as a shortcoming and feel that it is undermining the DO mezcal. Many are abandoning the designation, while some excellent new brands have decided to label themselves as agave spirits rather than mezcal.

Beyond Mexico: The New Centers of Agave

Demand for quality spirits has surged since the pandemic lock-downs. Tequila and mezcal were the second-fastest growing spirit category in 2022. However, under Mexican laws and DOs, both are proprietary spirits, and trade agreements between the United States and Mexico are cognizant of that fact. To be called tequila, a spirit must contain at least 51% Blue Weber agave and be made in Jalisco, Mexico. The same holds for mezcal; only producers in Mexican states that fall under the DO can call their distillations mezcal (Taxin, 2023).

Nature abhors a vacuum. and so does the world of commerce. When there is demand, a supply will be found. This is starting to happen in parts of the United States, where local producers look to fulfill demand. Some saw the gap a while ago and started growing agave; they are now harvesting their piñas. Others are importing agave or agave nectar from Mexico for their distillations. As mentioned previously, the succulent thrives in dry climates such as that of the southwestern United States. Entrepreneurs and aficionados alike are newly seizing on the opportunity to grow this drought-resistant crop. As increasing regulations limit groundwater extraction, local farmers are looking for more water-efficient crops. Cyclical patterns of drought and flooding also favor natural desert flora, perfectly suited to water famine followed by refreshing storms. As their Mexican counterparts before them, increasing numbers of growers are contemplating the planting of agave, a naturally occurring desert plant that requires almost no water once established. Some have already started.

Taking a leaf out of Mexico's book, California has enacted laws to protect this new industry. California agave spirits must be made exclusively from agave grown in the state and are to contain no additives.

In 2022, a number of growers and distillers joined together to form the California Agave Council, a voluntary and non-profit trade association (californiaagave.org).

I expect farmers in other states to develop their own cooperatives in the years to come. Arizona, Nevada, New Mexico, Texas, and Utah are all excellent candidates as they feature favorable terroirs and have wide open spaces to support rising demand for agave spirits.

Colorado is enjoying a boom in agave spirit production. One producer is using agave nectar imported from Mexico to make silver, gold, and extra-aged versions of agave spirits. Another uses Blue Weber agave that has been certified by state authorities as 100% organic and free trade to produce blanco and aged versions of its distillations. Still other Colorado producers are using agave imported from Mexico to make spirits containing 100% Blue Weber agave, as well as ones blended with sugarcane and other spirits.

The United States is a welcome entrant to the agave marketplace. Featuring exciting, distinct terroirs, researched production methods, and engaging family stories, American mezcaleros can be proud of their work and their innovative drinks' unique profiles. For example, agave plantations in the Rio Grande Valley of Texas feature a semi-arid climate which is much more humid than Sonora, and close to sea level rather than at the heady elevation of Zacatecas. Mexico has nothing to fear from the expansion of agave cultivation in new appellations, as agave spirits are a delicate reflection of the terroirs which produce them. Nobody can precisely replicate a mezcal from Oaxaca, and that means there is plenty of room for variety!

It takes time to scale up an industry based on a perennial crop. Sourcing agave while waiting for plants to mature can be a challenge for some, but for others the solution is surprisingly simple. It is found on many landowners' doorsteps: sotol. In Texas, the desert spoon plant is considered a weed. It seeds prolifically, animals don't eat it, and it grows across large parts of the state. Now ranchers are finding a new, lucrative use for these formerly annoying plants. Sotol is as diverse as agave—it has at least sixteen varieties. Early Americans were fabricating spirits from these plants as far back as ten thousand years ago. Sotol is also a very sustainable option, as its roots can be left in the ground, enabling the plants to grow again. Finally, the organic waste from production has many beneficial uses on ranches (Emen, 2019).

The arid regions of the U.S. Southwest aren't the only places considering agave spirits. In Queensland, Australia, farmers are growing fields of Blue Weber agave that rival those in Mexico. The Australian Agave Project is cultivating over five hundred thousand plants and plans to build a distillery (Brown, 2022). Its agave spirit is bold, with notes of citrus and grass.

South Africa's semi arid Karoo region is a great place to grow agave. It is known for its endless vistas, quirky towns, game reserves, ancient fossils, lamb, and honey. Since 2016, it has been adding agave spirits to the list. In early 2023, one Karoo agave spirit distiller, who follows a traditional Mexican recipe, received her own DO. *Agave americano* grows in the Karoo, so that's what most producers use, although others import their agave from Mexico (Van Deventer, 2021).

A word of caution: wherever you source your agave and whether you experiment with traditional recipes, producing the spirit just for yourself and a few friends or starting a commercial venture of any size, remember that you won't be able to legally call it mezcal or tequila unless you are doing so within certain Mexican states, as discussed earlier in this chapter.

Now that you've learned more about agave spirits and the laws governing their labels, it's time to find out more about the regions of Mexico where mezcal is produced. The next two chapters will focus on Oaxaca and other regions.

OAXACA IN A GLASS

> *I came to Oaxaca for mezcal. I like mezcal more and more these days.*

— ANTHONY BOURDAIN

> *There are places in the world that may be as beautiful as Oaxaca, but none more so.*

— FAUSTO ZAPATA

Because mezcal is a traditional drink deeply rooted in Mexican culture and tradition, this chapter, together with Chapter 6, aims to immerse you in the geography and landscape of Oaxaca and other parts of Mexico where mezcal is produced. This will enable you to appreciate the traditions that underpin mezcal-making.

MEZCAL MYTHS AND LEGENDS

The first paper mill wasn't introduced in Mexico until the 16th century, so we have to rely on oral histories to get an idea of what happened in the distant past. The Olmec culture was one of the oldest in *Mesoamerica*, lasting until around 400 B.C. Eventually the Olmecs were displaced by the Zapotecs, whose empire lasted until around 1000 A.D. when the more warlike Aztec and Mixtec peoples conquered much of their land. By the 16th century, when the Spanish encountered the Zapotecs in their Oaxacan redoubt, they gave them little heed as the surviving Zapotecs, in their remote mountain villages, did not present much of a threat to the outsiders. Across a history in which so many civilizations faded into the archaeological record, the Zapotecs are to be commended for their tenacity. Incredibly, the Zapotecs have been able to preserve their language from ancient times to the present day in the states of Oaxaca and Veracruz.

As the land changed hands over the centuries, warriors and farmers alike refreshed themselves with the delectable nectar of the agave. There are some wild legends about the origins of agave spirits, starting with the Zapotec story of the agave goddess Mayatl, who was renowned for her forty thousand leaves or breasts (depending on how much pulque one had to drink).

A Zapotec legend tells of this emotionless, sober, but very generous goddess. Mayatl's body was the trunk of the agave, and instead of leaves, she had forty thousand breasts (Cheung, 2021). Mezcal flowed from these and was reverently imbibed by those who venerated her. One day, worms burrowed into Mayatl's heart and became trapped inside for all time. The worms somehow became a revelation for Mayatl, who fell in love with Chag, a handsome but rather timid warrior. Although Chag cared deeply for Mayatl, he felt unworthy of her affections and prepared to leave her. In desperation, the goddess offered Chag one of her largest breasts so he could drink the mezcal which flowed from it. Chag did so without hesitation and became inebriated. In his altered state, he begged her to either turn him into a woman or make him into a god. Unfortunately, that's where the story ends. We will never know what happened after that!

Let us now turn to the account of the lovely Aztec goddess named Mayahuel. Both names, Mayatl and Mayahuel, are related to the word *maguey*, which as mentioned earlier, means agave.

To the Aztecs, Mayahuel was the goddess of the maguey. Two main stories about her are extant. In the first tale, she was a beautiful but lonely girl, long held captive by her grandmother in a far corner of the universe. She was eventually carried down to earth by Quetzalcoatl, the wind god, in a dance of passion. After several exciting episodes culminating in the evil grandmother's revenge and the destruction of Mayahuel, Quetzalcoatl had the last word: he transformed what was left of Mayahuel into a plant with many breasts or leaves, so that the Aztec people could remember and enjoy her forever.

In the second tale, Mayahuel was the woman who first thought of using the sweet sap of the agave, and her husband was the man who first used the succulent to make a medicine called pulque. This achievement earned the mythical couple a god and goddess designation, along with impressive claims. Mayahuel became the goddess of fertility and her children the gods of intoxication.

MEZCAL PRODUCTION: A SHORT HISTORY

Long before colonization and perhaps for centuries, indigenous peoples in Mexico were drinking fermented alcoholic beverages. Most of these were based on ingredients like agave, cornstalks, cactus fruits, maize, mesquite pods, honey, and even the bark of certain trees. By 2,000 B.C. and in common with people in other parts of the world, Mexico's Otomi people had developed a low-alcohol, fermented beverage that was drunk at religious ceremonies. The Otomi libation continued to be consumed by all the peoples who came after them, including the Olmecs, Zapotecs, and Mixtecs—who lived where Oaxaca is today—together with the Toltecs and Aztecs, who replaced them and ruled the nation from 1325 A.D. (Franklin, 2023).

One special fermented drink, consumed for century upon century, was derived from agave. We call it pulque, a shortened form of *octli poliuhuqui* in Nahualt, the language of the Aztecs. In pre-colonial Mexico, pulque was considered a sacred mixture, often with medicinal properties, and was often given to the elderly and nursing mothers. The ruling classes drank it during celebrations, ceremonies, and festivals.

When we project our feelings onto a hypothetical canvas of ancient Mexico, we may smile at deities like Mayahuel and shudder at a dreadful sun god, Huitzilopochtli, whom the Aztecs believed they had to placate with human blood. Indeed, the conquerors who constructed magnificent pyramids across Mexico routinely tortured and executed numerous slaves and prisoners of war. They thought that without regular, large-scale human sacrifice, the world would end. For this reason, powerful Aztec warriors would try to keep their enemies alive on the field of battle in order to march them to Tenochtitlan, along with some of the children and adults they captured in the conquered cities and settlements. These, they would subject to ritual sacrifice. The rest would be allowed to live, in exchange for allegiance and the payment of tribute.

The 16th century *Tribute Roll* or *Matrícula de tributos* is an impressive example of the recordkeeping practices the Aztecs used to monitor the tax payments of their subjugated peoples. The detailed documents were handwritten on *amate*, which is a paper made from tree bark. Drawings showed the items and quantities due from different villages, and the young men who would be conscripted as all males who were not slaves were required to attend systematic training and perform military service. We are fortunate to have copies of Tribute Rolls which were transcribed under the orders of Hernán Cortés, who wished to learn more about the Aztec society and economy. You can view this in the National Anthropological Library or *Biblioteca Nacional de Antropología* in Mexico City.

Tenochtitlan was the political and religious capital of the Aztec Empire, situated in the center of modern-day Mexico City. The Aztecs selected the spot to build their city-state, when they saw an eagle eating a snake atop a cactus.

The contemporary flag of Mexico commemorates this event with a centrally positioned coat of arms featuring a golden eagle biting down on a rattlesnake while perched on a prickly pear cactus! This representation alloys the salient Aztec legend with a traditional Spanish coat of arms, uniting the nation in a rich multicultural expression.

Starting in 1519, the Tlaxcaltec people (from Tlaxcala, which is the tiniest state in modern Mexico) allied themselves with the invading Spanish in a bid to defeat the Aztecs. Before the alliance was forged, the Tlaxcaltec people gained concessions from the Spanish to preserve most of their territory, and the Spanish honored these agreements across three centuries of colonial rule. This turned out to be a very wise decision for both sides! The autonomy of Tlaxcala was so ironclad that after Mexico gained independence from Spain in 1821, Tlaxcala remained sovereign as a federal territory. This lasted until Tlaxcala's admission to the Mexican union as a state in 1857.

Indeed, the Mesoamerican city-states were freed from the repressive reign of the Aztecs by Spanish commander Hernán Cortés and his conquistadors, who had arrived in Mexico in 1519.

The successful invasion of Cortés inaugurated the Spanish colonial era in Mexico, which lasted from 1521–1821. The conquest of the Aztecs held major geopolitical significance for the Spanish, who expanded their overseas colony called *New Spain* (officially the Viceroyalty of New Spain or *Virreinato de Nueva España*) to encompass an ambitious swath of the western hemisphere. At its zenith, the boundaries of New Spain extended from southern Oregon to Rock Springs, Wyoming, from Houston to Venezuela, and from Florida to the Greater Antilles. When one included old Spain, Spanish Guinea, the Philippines, Ecuador, Peru, and the southern cone of South America, it was a point of Spanish pride that they had birthed an empire where the sun never set.

The Spanish colonists struggled at first to adapt to life in Mesoamerica. They flocked to the cooler climates of the Mexican highlands and imported familiar foods and beverages, including wine and olive oil, from Europe (Franklin, 2023).

The Spanish considered pulque and its drinking barbaric. One of their concerns was the role that pulque played in local festivals and ceremonies, at times inciting its users to foment rebellions against them. Some Spanish officials even blamed indigenous insurrections on pulque. To maintain control of the colonies, the Spanish instituted regulations on pulque sales. They tried to shut down or limit *pulquerías*, pulque-serving taverns typically run by poor Spanish or *mestiza* women. Although Spanish rules crushed a few of these small businesses, many brave women persisted in carrying on the pulque trade and preserving their livelihood. The Spanish expanded their mandate to restrict agave cultivation, with very little success. Happily, it turns out that it's very hard to block access to something that grows naturally in the wild!

Some 50 years after the conquistadors set foot on Mexican soil, Filipino porcelain, silk, and spices were being ferried in giant *galleons* across the Pacific from Manila in the Philippines to Acapulco in Mexico, along a lucrative, twelve-thousand mile trade route (Franklin, 2023). Once on *terra firma*, the merchandise was loaded onto pack mules that would haul it across the Sierras and all the way to Veracruz for shipping to Spain, all in exchange for Mexican silver. Conditions on the galleons were horrific and many sailors died. Not surprisingly, numerous Filipino sailors abandoned their ships when they got to Mexico, bringing with them tamarind, rice, mangoes, coconuts, and the small stills they used for making coconut brandy. In the 17th and 18th centuries, Spanish settlers began experimenting with distillation of agave extracts, creating both early versions of mezcal and of alcoholic beverages made from sugar cane and coconut (Cheung, n.d.).

As for the Filipinos, they were by then integrated into the local Mexican population and made a low-alcohol beverage from palm sap called *tuba*, which is still sold today in Colima, Guerrero, Nayarit, Jalisco, Michoacán, and Oaxaca. The Filipinos had established coconut palm farms and begun distilling the tuba into a traditional drink called *lambanog*. The stills may have been simple affairs, unlike those imported by the Spanish, but the Filipinos used their specialized knowledge to distill agave liquors, especially in the mountains near modern Jalisco.

Because of the tremendous variety of agave species found around present-day Oaxaca, the region came to be known for its quality mezcals, with the different agaves delivering numerous flavor profiles. Mezcal became an important component of the local economy and culture, as it was made by small family-owned businesses employing traditional methods and tools. When in 1595, King Philip II of Spain established new restrictions on Mexican wine production (Franklin, 2023), local farmers focused less on planting new grapes and more on exploiting the agave.

Because of the tremendous variety of agave species found around present-day Oaxaca, the region came to be known for its quality mezcals, with the different succulents delivering numerous flavor profiles. Mezcal became an important component of the local economy and culture, as it was made by small family-owned businesses employing traditional methods and tools. When in 1595, King Philip II of Spain established new restrictions on Mexican wine production (Franklin, 2023), local farmers focused less on planting new grapes and more on exploiting the agave.

This paved the way for the establishment of Mexico's mezcal industry. In 1619, the locals were making an indigenous drink they called *mexcale* (Franklin, 2023). The novel beverage was distributed along the old trade routes and throughout the new Spanish mining settlements. Pedro Sánchez de Tagle, the Second Marquis of Altamira, even decided to build a large agave distillery in the town of Tequila, replacing mallets with tahonas to crush the roasted agave. In the meantime, Filipino stills were being used across a wide front, from Michoácan and Guerrero to Oaxaca, Zacatecas, and Durango. In Chihuahua, the locals were making sotol. Mescalero Apaches were also making their versions of mezcal in northern Mexico and what is now the Southwest United States.

The Spanish eventually banned mezcal production altogether. Producers were quick to relocate into the highlands, taking their portable stills with them, and thereby evading colonial officials. In the mountains, they also discovered more agave species with which to make mezcal. The ban was unsuccessful; mezcal was still being sold in Guadalajara in 1643, for example. Despite the ban, many families persisted in their business ventures. The Cuevos, for instance, were prominent agave spirits producers between 1740 and 1758 (Franklin, 2023). Imagine what it would have been like to sip a copita of bootleg mezcal on a bustling street in what was then Nueva Galicia!

In 1785, the Spanish King, Carlos III banned all alcohol production in New Spain in a *mercantilist* bid for Old Spain to dominate the market for alcoholic beverages. As a result, mezcal producers literally went underground. They began roasting agaves in underground pits, which produced the distinctive smokiness that characterizes so many mezcals today. In 1792, King Ferdinand IV finally lifted the ban and started taxing producers instead. This encouraged experimentation in the quest for improved versions of the spirit. By the 1870s, the mezcal produced in the Tequila-Guadalajara area had become sought-after due to its superior quality (Franklin, 2023).

The 19th century was a turbulent time in Mexico, as unrest and wars broke out across the country. In the 1850s, a shortage of firewood around Jalisco forced mezcal producers to devise steam-heated, aboveground ovens which reduced the smokiness of their mezcals, and modern tequila was born. Producers also began using commercial yeast strains rather than relying on wild ones.

In 1870, the Mexican government gave permission for these producers to call their product "tequila" and Blue Weber agave was chosen as the main species for use in its production. Tequila went from strength to strength in the intervening years, expanding its footprint and even winning awards at the Chicago World's Fair in 1873. As some tequila producers started more mechanized production methods to increase yields, their market grew. The Prohibition era in the United States further increased demand for the spirit as alcohol drinkers sought substitutes for their favored drinks (Franklin, 2023). Mezcal, tequila's country cousin, lagged far behind. Its production was banned in many areas after inferior goods entered the market (Franklin, 2023).

During the Mexican Revolution, mezcal united Mexicans and their traditions. Bottles appeared on tables at strategic meetings and gatherings, a symbol of the independent Mexican state. In 1994, mezcal received its own DO. The rest, as they say, is history.

MEZCAL WORMS: A MARKETING PLOY

Some bottles of mezcal contain unexpected hitchhikers—small, red or beige worms. Although they're often referred to as *gusanos de maguey* or agave worms, these worms are actually the larvae of a moth that lays its eggs on agave plants. They contribute little to mezcal flavors, and adding a worm to a bottle of mezcal isn't a Mexican tradition. It is an excellent marketing tool nevertheless, and if you're a producer, it will certainly ensure that consumers notice your brand.

The practice has its roots in a whisky shortage in the United States during World War II (Ellenwood, 2023). At the time, tequila was much easier to come by, and its popularity surged. Unable to cope with the sudden demand, tequila producers combed Mexico looking for mezcal producers who could fill the gap. In those days, most mezcal producers weren't very commercially minded and their spirits weren't branded or labeled. Enterprising Oaxacan producers added worms to their bottles to differentiate their drinks from mezcals produced elsewhere in Mexico.

In early 2023, U.S. researchers traveled to Oaxaca to find out exactly which insect's larva is present in mezcal bottles (Pinson, 2023). To their surprise, all the worms in the bottles turned out to be the reddish-colored larvae of agave redworm moths. White varieties, the researchers discovered, were simply ones that had been pickled in the alcohol for a longer period of time.

Is harvesting the worms harmful to the agave? It seems not. So-called maguey worms have been harvested as a delicacy since the days of the Aztecs, and yet the worms—as well as the host on which they feed—are thriving as never before.

OAXACA: THE HUB OF MEXICAN MEZCAL PRODUCTION

Bordering the Pacific Ocean in southern Mexico, Oaxaca nestles in a valley within the Sierra Madre mountains. The access roads are lined with agave plantations, the spiky, blue-green leaves of the plants reaching skyward. The town is the hub of Mexican mezcal production, with around 90% of the country's mezcal being produced here (The Origins of Oaxaca Mezcal, n.d.).

The Unique Terroir of Oaxaca

One reason why Oaxaca is ideal for mezcal production is that its terroir is one of the best in the country for agave, enabling superior plants to flourish. Oaxaca is a center of biodiversity. Numerous agave varieties grow naturally around the town; others thrive on plantations where they are skillfully cultivated. This means that Oaxacan mezcals are among the best.

For years, farmers have relied upon agaves to anchor the fragile desert soils, restore degraded lands, and break up compacted soils. Agave are pioneer plants, which means they prepare the land for later colonization by other plants or for cultivation. They stabilize soils on slopes and shelter less robust agricultural crop plants.

At just over 5,000 feet (1,550 meters) above sea level and surrounded by mountains, Oaxaca enjoys a climate that makes it ideal for agave cultivation and mezcal production. It's one of the most arid regions for its latitude in North America. This is because the mountains create a shield against the prevailing winds that carry moisture from the tropics. To give you an idea of how that influences Oaxaca's climate, other parts of Mexico at the same latitude (17 °N) receive more than five times the annual rainfall of Oaxaca. Along the same latitude, the Caribbean island of Nevis is lush and tropical, for example, but Oaxaca is more like the arid regions of the U.S. Southwest (The Editors of Encyclopedia Britannica, 2023).

The altitude reduces the heat that covers the tropical lowlands like a blanket all year. The thinner mountain atmosphere results in relatively cold nights, and it's even necessary to wear jackets on winter mornings, which is rare in much of Mexico.

One of the factors that make agave growing around Oaxaca so productive is the fact that the soils where certain varietals, such as *Agave angustifolia* and *Agave espadin* grow support beneficial bacteria that solubilize phosphorus, one of three essential nutrients for plant growth (the others are nitrogen and potassium). These bacteria are particularly prevalent in *montane* environments. A 2018 study found that these bacterial strains are genetically diverse and postulated that they could be used as biofertilizers and applied to plant root zones (Martínez-Gallegos et al., 2018).

Mezcal's Effects on Culture and Economy in Oaxaca

The streets of Oaxaca are lined with *mezcalerias*, small, family-owned bars where owners proudly serve local mezcals, including ones they've produced themselves. Bartenders and owners gladly share the histories of their particular spirits with their patrons, enabling them to find a mezcal to their taste. These bars usually stock only mezcal, and ordering anything else is frowned upon.

Mezcal is an important part of the local culture and is consumed at parties, weddings, and funerals. If someone has a hard day or is reeling from a bad experience, friends will suggest a little mezcal to restore spirits, add perspective, or dull the pain. An important festival where mezcal takes center stage is the Day of the Dead, which begins on October 31. On that day, the spirits of the dead are believed to join the living, with everyone drinking mezcal. Many families place bottles of mezcal and glasses on small altars in their living rooms.

Paralleling the upward trends in mezcal production and sales, tourism has increased dramatically as demand and curiosity about the spirit reach beyond Mexico's borders. In Oaxaca, this has provided economic spin-offs for all manners of vacation rentals, hotel rooms and other accommodations, as well as for artisan boutiques, exotic food markets, restaurants, and bars. Local producers also have ample opportunity to sell the much-heralded mezcal in its place of origin. Burgeoning and expanding brands alike need more workers and materials such as bottles, closures, labels, handmade paper, artwork supplies and gift boxes. Artists provide logos and illustrations. Wordsmiths write stories about the products. Other business opportunities abound. Tour guides escort visitors into the surrounding area to sample the cuisine and call on the manifold distilleries, describing the individual approaches to mezcal making. Further afield, they guide eager tourists wishing to explore the scenic mountains, view the 'water-fall' rock formations (*Hierve el Agua*), or visit ancient archaeological sites. People who provide these services, and those who support their household needs, all benefit from the boom.

There is also a burgeoning market for things that mezcal-makers discard, which have become trendy decor items—the wooden mallets used before tahonas came about, discarded clay fermentation and storage pots, piñas from which pulque juice has been extracted, rusty metal condensers, iron implements once used to cut agave, obsolete tools, and even vintage postcards. Demand for mezcal collectibles and antiques is creating another revenue stream for Oaxaca, further fueling its tourist industry. For those who can't make the trip, new entrepreneurs are selling these items online.

Bartenders, mixologists, restaurateurs, and online mezcal store owners are traveling to Oaxaca and other production centers to learn more about how agave spirits are made and what makes each batch unique. The melding of Oaxaca, mezcal, culture, and tradition needs to be experienced firsthand: YouTube videos can only do so much.

This has spawned a new craft industry, the creation of Oaxaca and mezcal-related tourist keepsakes—everything from hand-embroidered T-shirts and woolen rugs with traditional designs to carved wooden figurines, stone jimadors, silver agave earrings, and clay souvenir pots. For mezcal enthusiasts, there are glasses, copitas, clay serving pitchers, table runners, coasters, and bottle carriers. The list keeps growing.

Those who come to immerse themselves in mezcal, agave, and local culture are not your average tourists. Occasional rumors of government warnings, potential unrest, and disease outbreaks rarely dissuade them. They come because of the allure of mezcal and the attraction of a culture that doesn't conform to the latest global trends. Perhaps they even view their stay as a visit to earlier, if not simpler, times. Whatever the case may be, they seize the opportunity to absorb Oaxacan traditions, experience Oaxaca's special flavors, and meet the people who create mezcal in their backyards. Back home, they may be viewed with envy. Mezcal is permeating the world's consciousness from New York and London to Sydney and Cape Town, and there are umpteen business prospects. The mezcal boom is a win-win. Oaxaca is the epicenter, poised to take advantage of every opportunity these meticulously crafted spirits produce.

SOME RENOWNED OAXACAN MEZCAL BRANDS

The tales behind these well-known brands epitomize the story of mezcal throughout Mexico. Many of today's industry leaders began as small and humble homegrown businesses with rudimentary marketing and few commercial outlets.

Real Minero

Real Minero dates back to the 19th century when the family started a small operation to supplement their meager income. Their ancestors had once hidden in the mountains to make mezcal after the Spanish outlawed its production. In 1978, the family finally acquired a palenque, one of the first in their area. Like many mezcal producers at the time, they decanted their spirits into plastic jugs and recycled bottles to be sold at a small store in Ocotlán. Rudimentary labels bearing the store's name were photocopied and glued onto the containers.

Only in 1999 did Real Minero get its first proper label, which was subsequently updated to include its logo. The labels were affixed to the square glass bottles mezcal producers were using at the time. In 2005, to comply with DO standards, Real Minero called its mezcal *joven*. Another label with proper branding was developed. To celebrate the palenque's thirtieth birthday, Real Minero released its first collector's edition, limited to just one hundred twenty bottles. In 2009, the brand started exporting its mezcal to Europe. In subsequent years, its label was updated, more collector's editions were released, and it began exporting to the United

States. More recently, Real Minero abandoned the DO standard due to the red tape involved and now calls its products agave spirits (Carreno, n.d.).

Rey Campero

Another family-owned brand, this mezcal is made by Romulo Sanchez, master mezcalero. Happily situated near the small Oaxaca town of Candelaria Yegolé, the family's property is surrounded by wild agaves, with a nearby river providing crystal clear water. The brand's pastoral location and many accolades echo its chosen name: Rey Campero, or King of the Countryside. Sanchez's great-grandmother founded the town and built its first palenque. Sanchez, who learned the trade from his father, relies on methods that date back to 1870. He uses Maguey Tobalá and blends other agave varieties in other batches. Flavor profiles and aromas are complex, tending toward intense spiciness with tropical fruit and herbal notes. Rey Campero entered the international market in 2012 and has won several awards. It plans to maintain its traditions to serve a growing fan base and is replanting native agaves to ensure their persistence in the wild and the future of mezcal (Producer Profile: Rey Campero Mezcal, 2018).

Siete Misterios Arroqueño

In 2010, this mezcal brand, the name of which means "the seven mysteries", was founded by two Mexican brothers, Eduardo and Julio Meistre, who quit their day jobs to follow their passions for mezcal and Mexico. They began by tasting as many Oaxacan-produced mezcals as they could, finding inspiration from successful, established mezcaleros and distillers, some of whom are now part of their "seven mysteries". The Meistre brothers use traditional production methods steeped in Mexican culture, distilling their mezcal in copper stills and clay pots. They use agaves found around Oaxaca for their young mezcals, which are distilled from 100% agave sugars. These exhibit diverse flavor profiles and smooth textures (Chatham Imports, 2023; Rooney, 2023; Siete Misterios, n.d.).

Lalocura Tobasiche-Espadín

Distilled in clay pots and using only traditional methods passed down through four generations of mezcal makers, Lalocura has built up a cult following. After working for many years as a master distiller for his family's brand and with a degree in agricultural engineering under his belt, master mezcalero Eduardo "Lalo" Angeles started Lalocura in 2014. He makes sure that farm workers are carefully taught about propagating and cultivating agaves and hires local craftsmen to make the distillery's traditional tools and equipment. People from far and wide join Lalo's neighbors to savor the mezcals at the family palenque. His mezcals are only available on a limited basis at a few Mexican outlets and are solidly welded to Mexican traditions and values (Lalo, 2018).

"La locura" in Spanish means "the madness" in English, so you can hear a fun pun in this name!

Mezcal Vago Elote

This mezcal is a love affair starring an ailing visitor, the kind and beautiful nurse who cared for him, and the mezcal her farmer father made on the side. Soon, with the help of a friend, Mezcal Vago was born. The brand's love story continues. It is visible in the three agaves planted for each harvested one. It is invisible, but very real, in each batch of additive free mezcal. It manifests itself in the simple, but colorful labels that playfully inform potential drinkers and buyers about Vago's four master mezcaleros and the excellent spirits they each farm in different parts of Oaxaca and produce according to their own individual techniques. It is heard in fun names like 'Vago Elote' or 'Lazy Corn', evoking the roasted corn added to this mezcal between the third and fourth distillations. The brand's spirits are entirely produced from cultivated and wild agave, and using traditional methods. Some are lightly filtered before bottling (Mezcal Vago, 2012).

Del Maguey Chichicapa (Single Village)

When he founded Del Maguey in 1995, visual artist Ron Cooper set out to foster some of Mexico's unique cultural lore. Selecting the name of the mythical agave goddess Maguey as a frame for his spirit collections was a start. Establishing close ties with Zapotec and Mixtec farmer-mezcaleros from remote corners of Oaxaca put the focus on rich ancestral traditions that highlight each single-village, handmade selection. The mezcals' success has created significant economic opportunities for the local population. In 2006, after a trip to visit mezcal-loving relatives in Chicago, Cooper created a lower-proof version for the U.S. market. Vida can be savored one drop at a time for its complex flavors, mixed into cocktails, or sipped neat from a copita. Traditionally produced, this brand and its success created a minor economic boom in its hometown of San Luis del Rio. The unique, eye-catching labels on its green glass bottles were designed by Cooper's long-time friend Kenneth Price and make Vida instantly recognizable. Even as demand necessitated that Del Maguey scale up production, the brand maintained both its cultural identity and environmental sustainability. Del Maguey is committed to the upliftment of the local community, holding workshops and providing educational and healthcare assistance. The brand is involved in reforestation efforts and cultivating wild agaves (Hank, 2019; History, Del Maguey, n.d.).

The Lost Explorer Mezcal

Far from a place of diminishing resources, The Lost Explorer gratefully receives nature's agave gift and confidently plants three replacements for each mature, harvested one, respecting the land's biodiversity. Because the brand handles every aspect of production, co-founders David de Rothschild and Thor Björgólfsson provide many sustainable jobs for fortunate Oaxacans who would otherwise leave Mexico's poorest state in search of work. Lost Explorer mezcals are produced by maestro mezcalero Don Fortino Ramos, who has been making and distilling mezcal the traditional way for over forty years. Made from espadin, tobalà, and salmiana agaves, the spirits are distilled on the outskirts of San Pablo Huixtepec, Oaxaca. These mezcals are defined by sweet, spicy flavors, with hints of smoke, fruit, herbs, and fresh agave (The Lost Explorer, n.d.).

Other Superior Oaxacan Mezcals

Many other excellent mezcals that are traditionally produced in and around Oaxaca have won acclaim beyond Mexico's borders. Here are a few (Shelley, 2024):

- **Illegal Mezcal Añejo** is made from espadin agave and is aged for thirteen months in oak barrels. Its 7 Year Añejo was aged for seven years in thirty-five barrels of French oak. It is said Illegal's founder John Rexer originally smuggled mezcal to his Guatemala bar.
- **Casamigos Joven** is a new mezcal, made from 100% agave espadin grown in Oaxaca and produced in the traditional

manner by fourth-generation mezcaleros. Bottles are handcrafted and each one is different. These mezcals have herbal, fruity aromas and notes of smoke and pepper. The name Casamigos, House of Friends, reflects the brand's founding and original ownership by George Clooney and friends.

- **Mezcal Bozal** is justly proud of its "wildly refined" mezcals, secured from agaves perilously harvested on abrupt hillsides and long prized by indigenous mescaleros. Bozal meticulously perpetuates a two-hundred-year tradition of mezcal making in earthen pots. Open-air fermentation allows natural yeasts to craft the spirits before double distillation purifies the fermented product. Wild-mountainside nursery plantings promise an agave-rich future.

- **Montelobos Mezcal**, founded by a fifth-generation mezcalero and a PhD in botany, combines practical knowledge passed down faithfully from parent to child and research-based expertise acquired from long study to uphold the highest levels of production competence and respect for the land and its people. Montelobos means Wolf Mountain. The name evokes the brand's efforts to protect and improve the ecosystem and the local families it employs. This is visible in its organic farming and sustainably-sourced mezcal production. It is also evidenced in the enriched living conditions Montelobos workers enjoy. While their daily experiences and prospects are far better than their forebears', they maintain the rich traditions and mezcal-production understanding that are part of their heritage.

- **Dos Hombres** produces both joven and tobalá mezcals made by blending quality agaves that are hand-selected from the countryside surrounding San Luis del Rio in

Oaxaca. The two American actors ("Two Men") who launched Dos Hombres knew that to create the spectacular mezcals they envisioned, they would need more than just a good distiller; they would need an artist. Maestro Gregorio Velasco is that artist. Since the age of 8, he has dedicated himself to bringing together the best agave and the finest traditional techniques in the pursuit of excellence. His small-batch mezcals are satisfyingly complex and reflect the history and beauty of the surrounding mountains.

- **Ojo de Tigre Mezcal Artesanal** is considered one of the best Mexican mezcals. A sweeter mezcal with complex herbal flavors, it is made from a combination of espadin and tobalá agaves harvested in Oaxaca and Puebla. *Ojo de Tigre* means Tiger's Eye, a semi-precious stone viewed by some ancient people as holding special powers and worn as an amulet. The brand's specially designed bottle winks at the traditional superstition by resembling *anforitas* treated as amulets in days of yore. This conjures up the mystical beginnings of mezcal and the mysterious traditions associated with the early people of Mexico.

- **Madre Mezcal** is handmade in the hills of Oaxaca by three families who once sold mezcal in plastic jugs or as plant-based medicine. This traditional use of the spirit goes back to the dawn of time, at least as far as oral histories, ethnology, and archaeology go. Today, Madre's certified mezcals draw on the best of ancient traditions. Mescaleros of old relied on the airborne yeast and the local water sources that still help bring about today's mezcals. Their open-air palenques and earthen ovens are similar to the ones Madre uses in its desire to achieve excellence and authenticity. Madre means mother, and the brand is faithful to its ancestry. Today, descendants of generations of mezcaleros plant, tend to, harvest, and bless their espadin and cuishe agaves. Besides mezcal, Madre offers a tempting range of sparkling, botanically inspired drinks. Madre Mezcal is now an international brand.

- **Alipus San Luis Del Rio** is not just a brand; it is a lifestyle. The multi-generational families of artisans who care for the land and its product live where they work, and work where they live. They grow up around the distilleries, lend a hand as soon as they're able, make their own tools, and understand every aspect of production. Venerable equipment is the norm in their old-fashioned operations. The success of their old-recipe mezcals preserves an endangered way of life. From the special terroir of San Luis del Rio, they harvest espadin agaves from which they capably craft an artisanal mezcal with rich, fruity flavors.

- **El Jolgorio Madrecuishe** is a fun mezcal brand, featuring bright labels inspired by festivals that take place in villages in the Oaxacan mountains. *Jolgorio* means celebration or revelry. When mezcal is present, the joy is contagious. Over sixteen families across Oaxaca contribute to the brand's mezcals. This one is produced from the rarely used madrecuishe agave, a high-elevation plant which imparts an unusual combination of floral, fruity, and mineral flavors, its complexity a festive challenge to the sipper.

- **Nuestra Soledad Santa Maria Zoquitlán** is produced in Zoquitlán, often regarded as an epicenter of mezcal production. Nuestra Soledad, our Solitude or Our Lady of Solitude, has been revered as a saint since the seventeenth century. The label honors her, as well as the values and traditions that have sustained the culture for centuries. The small town of Santa María Zoquitlán is flanked by two river valleys where rare agave varieties thrive on steep hillsides. Ignacio "Don Chucho" Parada, master mezcalero, and his son José produce this joven mezcal from espadin agave harvested on the slopes. The traditionally crafted spirit boasts aromas of lemon, tropical fruit, and smoked game, a complex, creamy palate, and a strong finish of stone fruit and savory herbs.

- **Los Amantes** offers different types of mezcal, each made by hand from individual batches of unique agaves. They are produced in Tlacolula de Matamoros, located in Oaxaca's Central Valley. Why do the bottles bear the mark NOM 001X? The answer is simple: Destilería Tlacolula was the first palenque to be certified by the mezcal regulation board. This goodwill toward modern institutions in no way belies the brand's association with mezcal's ancestral story. The motto "Tradition, Art, and Innovation" aptly describes Los Amantes, as it aspires to strike a balance between beneficial progress and rich tradition. Earthen pits, a stone mill, copper stills, and French oak barrels are used to produce the mezcal. "Los Amantes" means "The Lovers" and refers to the Aztec legend wherein Quetzalcoatl wept on the grave of his lover Mayahuel, thus enabling the growth of the maguey plant from which mezcal was made.

- **Mezcal de Leyendas**, or Mezcal of Legends, produces mezcals from an exceptional variety of agaves, some of them new to mezcal aficionados. Although the word "legend" has traditional connotations, Leyendas is famous for innovation. The company may be the first to rely entirely on solar energy to run its operation and is proud of its other sustainable initiatives. It uses a solar-run steam-heated steel oven, mechanical grinder, and copper alembic still. Fermentation is in oak wood tanks.

- **Pensador Mezcal**, or the Thinker's Mezcal, evokes a time when one could think with fewer distractions, because once away from human villages, the main noise interruptions came from sources such as the wind and rain or birds flying overhead. The wind once blew over a Nahuatl-speaking settlement the people had named "The Place of the Ear of Corn" (Miahuatlán). Later, when it went by, other Aztecs had taken over, and later still, the Spaniards. The years passed. Agaves grew. Mezcal was made. Today, when Don Atenogenes and his family make Pensador Mezcal near Miahuatlán, Oaxaca, they uphold the heritage that is theirs. From a harvest of proven espadin and madrecuishe, they slowly hand make a superb, aromatic mezcal, using traditional methods their ancestors perfected in the sixteenth century.

- **Santo Mezquila** is an unusual spirit that combines mezcal and tequila. It is a blend of 100% Blue Weber agave tequila from Jalisco and 100% espadin agave mezcal from Oaxaca. Mezquila brings together two previously estranged spirits, each with its own birthright. The marriage is smooth, with an earthy, herbal flavor and smoky notes.

While Oaxaca's unique geography and climate, as well as its well-deserved reputation in both mezcal-making culture and tourism, make it the epicenter of mezcal production in Mexico, there are other places where this alluring spirit is made. In the next chapter, you'll find out more about them.

Bebí de tu memoria
Aroma a tierra, agave y sol
Yo soy la que le gusta
Este castigo mejor
Gota, gota, gota, gotita de mezcal
Gota, gota, gota, gotita de mezcal

I drank in your memory
Aroma of earth, agave and sun
I am the one who likes it
This punishment is better
Drop, drop, drop, droplet of mezcal
Drop, drop, drop, droplet of mezcal

- Lila Downs, "Mezcalito"

BEYOND OAXACA: MEZCAL ACROSS MEXICO

> *South of the border, down Mexico way. That's where I fell in love, where stars above came out to play. And now as I wander, my thoughts ever stray south of the border, down Mexico way.*
>
> — JIMMY KENNEDY

> *Civilization begins with distillation.*
>
> — WILLIAM FAULKNER

This chapter will introduce you to mezcal production outside of the Oaxaca region.

MEZCAL PRODUCTION IN OTHER MEXICAN STATES

As mentioned previously, mezcal has a denomination of origin (DO) for nine Mexican states: Durango, Guerrero, Guanajuato, Michoacán, Oaxaca, Puebla, San Luis Potosí, Tamaulipas, and Zacatecas.

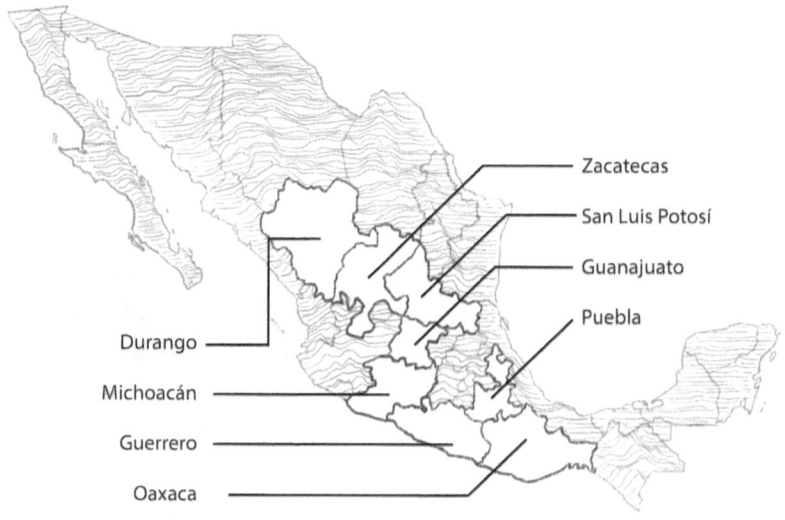

Durango

Situated in northern Mexico, Durango produces superior mezcals that are on par with those from Oaxaca, although the regions' cultures and traditions differ. To begin with, mezcal producers in Durango use their own terms to describe the people and places related to mezcal-making. A mezcalero in Oaxaca is referred to as a *vinatero* in Durango, for instance, while a palenque is called a *vinata*.

Here, the agave most commonly used in mezcal production is *Agave durangensis*, which is abundant in the wild. The locals have named it cenizo or "ash" because of its gray-green color. Other agaves used include *Agave bovicornuta* (masparillo) and *Agave angustifolia* (tepemete), together with several lesser-known varieties.

The landscapes of Durango are a mosaic of forests, mountains, and deserts. Forests cover large tracts of land, so vinateros have many different types of wood to choose from when it comes to making fires in their roasting pits. Permits are required to harvest any naturally occurring wood, although distilleries situated in very remote areas may be exempt from this requirement. Many producers use encino, a type of oak, and mesquite. The latter produces copious amounts of smoke when it burns, increasing the smoky flavor of the mezcal.

Durango's mezcal production differs from Oaxaca's in other ways. The roasted piñas are crushed by hand with mallets rather than with tahonas turned by donkeys or horses. It's back-breaking work, and the mallets are surprisingly heavy. Only two of Durango's many mezcal brands use a tahona, and both have Oaxacan links.

Fermentation tubs are also distinctive in Durango. They are neither vats nor clay pots, but oblong boxes set into the ground. They are usually insulated with mud or clay and then lined with wood. This helps to stabilize fermentation temperatures and protects the contents while allowing them to be exposed to oxygen in the air.

Durango's mezcal producers only went commercial in the early 2000s; some of its old brands are a mere fifteen years old. In 2017, the state produced less than 2% of Mexican mezcals. The following year, the Durango Mezcal Cluster was formed to formalize the industry in Durango. Twenty of the state's largest producers have joined the Cluster and thirty more have applied for membership. The group aims to penetrate new markets and help smaller operations obtain certification (Lampert, n.d.; Delamater, 2022).

Consumers need to know that Durango's version of mezcal typically has a higher alcohol content than its Oaxacan counterpart. This is in keeping with its particular production techniques and the fact that they have been virtually unchanged for a century (Thelmadatter, 2022). Adjustments and innovations are likely to appear in the future, especially as new distilleries stake their claims. The growing market will also encourage adjustments. Some Durango businesses will continue to make their spirits the old-fashioned way, while others will strive to meet different customer preferences.

Durango Mezcal Brands

- Ajal
- Burrito Fiestero
- Casa Volador
- Cutwater Spirits
- La Remilgosa
- La Tierra de Acre
- Lamata
- Legendario Domingo
- Leyendas Vinata
- Maguey Melate
- Origen Raiz del Espiritu
- Rao Senco
- Ultramundo

Guerrero

The region ranks second after Oaxaca in the volume of mezcal it produces. In 2021, this volume reached around 396,258 gallons (1.5 million liters) a year, providing an excellent revenue stream not just for the state, but also for the people. Indeed, agave management and mezcal production benefit more than the individuals who are directly involved in the industry and their families; they allow those who sell them needed supplies and those who work at meeting the overall needs of the community to improve their living conditions, sometimes significantly. When tourists let their sense of adventure and the tantalizing words on a mezcal-bottle label guide them to previously undiscovered areas, they become partners with the local people in fostering the growth of the area's economy. It is good to remember that many a thriving village started with a resilient, but struggling population. The exploding interest in mezcal consumption and the growing appeal of mezcal tourism equals economic opportunity.

Guerrero also boasts the second-highest number of agave-spirit producers in Mexico (La Luna Mezcal, 2021). Many enterprises are based in small towns scattered across the state, and visiting them is a far more adventurous affair than touring Oaxaca distilleries, as mezcal tourism is virtually non-existent in Guerrero. If you are an intrepid traveler and wish to witness the place before it is further developed, prepare yourself! You may feel like you're intruding onto an exciting film set or are experiencing a thrilling return to another time. Rutted roads are choked with chickens and other livestock, straw is everywhere, and—to Western eyes at least —things appear rather disorganized. You'll definitely need to take more than just a packed lunch before embarking on your adventure! The infrastructure and facilities may be spare, but the people can be extraordinarily hospitable, and the incredible mezcal they produce will make the expedition worthwhile. If you would like to observe agave farmers at work, you should be aware that most of the labor takes place outside of the summer rainfall season.

Agave cupreata (maguey papalote or ancho) is mainly used for mezcal production, together with *Agave angustifolia guerensis* (zacatoro). These are harvested from the surrounding countryside, where they grow prolifically.

One of the big differences between the production styles of Guerrero and Oaxaca is that in the former the piñas are roasted right where the agaves are harvested, whereas in the latter they are transported to the palenque for processing. In Guerrero, rocks and firewood are abundant and it is much easier to roast onsite than to haul the piñas to a separate processing facility. New rocks are used at every harvest and a specialist *fogonero* oversees the roasting. After the piñas are added to the pit, they are covered with palm fronds and sand before being left to roast for around ten to fifteen days (Glueck, 2019). The team leaves the piñas to their processing and returns when the time has come to remove and transport them back to the palenques—called *fábricas* in Guerrero—for fermentation in traditional wooden vats, followed by distillation in copper stills. Transportation during and after production significantly increases costs for mezcal-makers.

Most mezcals are around 50%–52% ABV, although you can get some at the fábricas that have an ABV as high as 75% (Ben & Anthony, n.d.; Glueck, 2019).

Guerrero Mezcal Brands

- Aguerrido
- Bozal
- Cinco Sentidos (5 Senditos)
- Clase Azul

- Cuentacuentos
- Derrumbes
- El Tigre
- Legendario Domingo
- Machetazo
- Maguey Melate
- Mal Bien
- Marca Negra
- Mezcalosfera de Mezcaloteca
- Mixtape
- Pelotón de la Muerte
- Rayo Seco
- Reyes y Cobardes
- Tecuán
- Tohue Tohue
- Tres Papalote

Guanajuato

This region is Mexican mezcal's hidden gem. While it doesn't immediately come to mind when you think of mezcal, it produces some unusual iterations, including a pink one. Guanajuato's climate and soil conditions create a unique terroir, producing mezcals with very distinct aromas and flavors. The state's centuries-old history, colorful traditions, and vibrant culture are reflected in its mezcals. The spirits' indigenous name was pulque; the Spanish nicknamed them *aguardiente*, or burning water. This term, fraught with humorous connotations, was not unique to the New World. It was commonly used on the Iberian Peninsula to describe several varieties of strong alcoholic drinks. Contemporary artisans still craft mezcals by following ancient recipes, and their spectacular spirits promote a growing interest in the region and its products.

Three varieties of locally occurring agave are used for mezcal. The most common is *Agave salmiana*, a large, robust plant that yields prolific nectar. Guanajuato's open spaces and fertile soils yield bold, earthy flavors with an underlying sweet smokiness. Another agave used is the rare, wild *Agave potatorum* (tobalá), which in Guanajuato confers sweet, floral flavors with mineral notes. Producers in the mountainous parts of the state harvest wild *Agave cupreata* (papalote) to make their fruity, spicy, and slightly acidic mezcals. They craft their mezcal according to popular traditional methods, by roasting the agave piñas in stone-lined earthen pits and crushing them by hand or with horse-drawn tahonas. Wooden barrels are mostly used for fermentation, while most mezcaleros in Guanajuato use pot stills for distillation.

Guanajuato's mezcal producers, mindful of the future of their industry, practice reforestation and minimize as much as possible their reliance on synthetic pesticides. In this dry region, many palenques have adopted water-saving practices to minimize limit water use. As part of their long-term perspective on cultivation, they plant different species of agave to promote biodiversity and balance regional ecology. When local people are involved or at least influential in decision making, they bring to the table a working familiarity with the natural ecosystem and a crucial understanding of the cultural environment. Within this context, they are better able to protect historical values and traditional resources while fostering essential improvements in a given business. Instead of being viewed by the public with suspicion or even hostility, a new employer has a golden opportunity to be welcomed by well-established families with deeply-rooted ties to their area.

Mezcal production, whether by the descendants of a region's first mezcaleros or by relative newcomers to a locality, can benefit entire communities. Higher wages are a boon to the local economy; the ensuing betterment of individual families strengthens existing businesses and attracts new ones. Producers also support educational initiatives that may transform the lives of those who take advantage of them.

One of the more recent developments in Guanajuato is the creation of Mezcal Routes in San Luis de la Paz and San Felipe. Tourists can now explore local distilleries and taste exciting mezcals. History lovers are in for a treat: some haciendas on the routes have been producing agave spirits for centuries! At each natural stopping place, there are colorful villages to be discovered, delicious fare to be sampled, inspiring tales to be heard, and antique structures to be glimpsed.

The route includes fine examples of historic architecture, such as the Cathedral de León and Juarez Theatre in San Felipe. In San Luis de la Paz, tours often include Pozos de Mineral, an abandoned mining town, and the pink stone cathedral Parroquia de San Miguel Arcangel. Regional food is served at mezcal tastings.

Guanajuato Mezcal Brands

- Hacienda Vergel de Guadalupe
- Jaral de Berrio
- Lucy Pistolas
- Maguey Melate
- Mezcal Chantaman
- Mezcal Penca and Stone
- Mezcal Rancho la Quinta
- Torres Mochas
- Villasuso

Michoacán

With its wealth of variety in agave species Michoacán is a thriving center of mezcal production, although as of this writing, few of these mezcals are exported internationally. The agaves most commonly used are *Agave cupreata* (chino), followed by *Agave inaequidens* (alto or bruno). *Agave cupreata* only grows on high ridges above the Balsas River, which divides Michoacán and Guerrero. The harvest season is short and frequently disrupted by the heavy summer rains that begin in June. While *Agave inaequidens* produces one of Michoacán's most superior mezcals, it takes fifteen years for the plant to mature and it has a very low sugar content, so a relatively large crop is required for production (Tomky, 2022).

Patience is needed before and after harvest, as the traditional methods of mezcal-making employed by local mezcaleros make production time-consuming:

After the agave is roasted, it is broken by hand with wooden mallets or mechanically with wood chippers. Because nights are cold in the region, the nectar is fermented in pits dug into the ground. Some sources allege that this practice is a hangover from the time when mezcal production was prohibited and palenques were routinely raided. Perhaps both are true! Underground pits can protect from both the cold and prying eyes. Be that as it may, pulque is sometimes added to the mixture (Lampert, 2019). Other particularities distinguish local mezcal-making practices. Whereas other regions of Mexico rely on copper alembic stills, Michoacán favors the use of wooden stills which promote internal condensation. Because wood is a far more insulating material than copper, the mezcal is quite hot when it emerges from the outlet tube. Copper binds sulfur as copper sulfate, whereas wood does not. This means that Michoacán's unique mezcals can bear faint traces of sulfur, which although undetectable to the human palate, sufficiently modify the drinker's perception of the aromatics to deliver a sublime flavor profile.

Michoacán's mezcals range from funky, high-alcohol tipples to fresh, salty, mineral-like spirits with a whiff of cucumber. They also tend to be less smoky than their Oaxacan cousins.

Because of Mexico's stringent certification requirements, few of the mezcals produced in Michoacán can be exported. Furthermore, the certifying body in Oaxaca initially argued against the specific traditional production methods used by many of Michoacán's mezcaleros, thus delaying the state's certification until 2012 (Tomky, 2022). However, the situation is brighter today. On the plus side, some municipalities are certified to produce both tequila and mezcal. Several self-governing alliances like the Union of Mezcal Producers of Michoacán have also appeared on the scene to assist producers with their certification and marketing needs.

Michoacán Mezcal Brands

- 5 Sentidos
- Don Mateo de la Sierra
- Hacienda Oponguio
- La Luna
- Legendario Domingo
- Leyendas
- Maguey Melate
- Mal Bien
- Mezonte
- Mixtape
- Pal'alma
- Palomas Mensajeras
- Siembra Metl

- Sin Gusano Project

Puebla

Although Puebla only joined the DO in 2015, its distillers have a long tradition of mezcal-making. Some are quick to point out that they were producing mezcal long before it became commonplace in Oaxaca. I will not take sides in the argument but congratulate both regions on their success in preserving ancient artisanal skills. One of the indicators of mezcal's long history in Puebla is the plethora of available brands and the indisputable experience of local mezcaleros, easily demonstrated in their superb spirits.

For tourists a visit to Puebla combines well with a trip to Oaxaca, as the two states border each other and afford the traveler some breathtaking mountain views. They boast a wide diversity of naturally occurring agaves, and exciting brands of mezcal are commonly available on both sides of their political boundary. In Puebla as in Oaxaca, small towns with a multitude of family-run distilleries abound, each with long lineages of producers spanning several generations (Lampert, 2022).

The premier agave used for mezcal production in Puebla is *Agave potatorum* (papalome or papalometl), known as tobalá in Oaxaca. The good news for locals is that this agave is much more common in Puebla than in Oaxaca. Pueblan mezcals derived from it have creamy, mineral flavors with floral, herbaceous notes. Another favorite is *Agave angustifolia*, Puebla's answer to espadin, a workhorse variety that results in fruity and spicy mezcals. Additional preferred varieties are *Agave cupreata*, which was originally cultivated in government plantations in the 1990s, and *Agave salmiana, which is* used for pulque. Puebla is also an emerging sotol producer, thanks to *Dasylirion lucidum* (cucharilla), an agave-like plant that also grows there.

Women dominate Puebla's mezcal industry and always have. They either grow agaves or process, distill, bottle, and sell mezcal. These women are increasingly recognized for their achievements and many brands proudly advertise the success of their female mezcaleros and owners.

As stated above the region has numerous mezcal brands, and a mezcal route was recently inaugurated to enhance visitor experiences. Mexico's Ministry of Tourism opened this Mezcal Route in 2021. The itinerary spans four municipalities in centers of mezcal production, offering opportunities to tour distilleries and enjoy mezcal tastings and other attractions (Meneses, 2021). Along the way, travelers can admire aesthetically pleasing fields of agave, learn from the growers who farm those fields, eat in the home of a local family, and admire colorful villages where life is still slow.

Puebla Mezcal Brands

- 5 Sentidos
- Cuish Pichumetl
- Del Maguey (Vida)
- El Destilado
- Fósforo
- Luneta
- Matuey Melate
- Montelobos
- Ojo de Tigre
- Pal'alma

San Luis Potosí

Located in central Mexico, this state is better known for its waterfalls and colonial architecture than its mezcal, although this is due to the fame of its scenic splendor and historic buildings, not to any perceived inferiority in the fruit of its agave. During the 19th century, San Luis Potosí was the silver-mining capital of Mexico, and many haciendas where mezcal is now produced date from that era. However, San Luis Potosí is a mezcal destination in its own right. Some of the best Mexican mezcals originate in this state, where they have been produced for at least five hundred years (Garrone, 2020). The survival of ancient traditions of mezcal making, such as the reliance on *Capacha* clay stills and millennia-old Mongolian production methods, testifies to the venerable age of artisanal mezcal crafting in San Luis Potosí. Echoes of 500 years of uninterrupted historical techniques are found in the old-style internal capture stills based on 16th century Filipino models. The industry suffered many ups and downs over the centuries, often mirroring (as it did elsewhere) the prevailing political conditions. Following the Mexican Revolution, for instance, production dwindled considerably. Without the ingenuity of persistent mezcaleros, it would have come to a standstill. It eventually made a rapid comeback and in recent years has grown far beyond expectations, with many mezcals winning awards that make the region proud.

One of the reasons for this accomplishment is that most of San Luis Potosí lies in Mexico's high desert, where there's little rainfall and soils are mineral-rich. The agaves, as other succulents, can survive with minimal moisture, and the desert environment creates a unique terroir for mezcals. Most of San Luis Potosí's bounty is produced from five varieties of *Agave salmiana* (blanco, bronco, chino, cuerno, and verde). *Agave salmiana is* a low-yielding species requiring more plants for mezcal production than some other varieties, but it is plentiful in the surrounding desert and easy to cultivate in adjacent climates.

Locals also produce their mezcals a little differently than most. Once the piñas are roasted and crushed, the juice is siphoned off to be fermented and distilled without the mash or mosto. Because of the desert's temperature variations, where broiling days give way to frigid nights, fermentation can be a challenging process. To help ensure proper fermentation, pulque is added to the pressed agave juice. This creates a different type of mezcal, one which thrills with its ripe pickle and jalapeño flavors.

As in other regions, most producers with foresight are mindful of their ongoing need for agave and practice reforestation. Planting two or even three agaves for each harvested one should ensure a steady supply in the foreseeable future, despite a significant increase in popularity. Demand for the succulent has intensified in recent years, ever since the agave nectar industry began competing for agave piñas with mezcal-makers. In 2019, as many as sixty thousand piñas a day were being transported to Jalisco to fuel this production, with no apparent plans for harvest controls or replanting (Coss, 2019). If this short-sighted approach describes the current reality, it must soon yield to sounder business practices. The nectar industry will need to join the mezcaleros in funding or practicing agave cultivation. It is a universally known fact that each year, vegetable farmers sow seeds to replace the produce they have harvested. It is a lesser known fact that in the United States, logging companies plant two-and-a-half trees for each one they harvest. This is done not simply out of love for the environment, but for the obvious reason that one cannot be a lumberjack or a farmer without trees or produce.

San Luis Potosí Mezcal Brands

- Campanilla
- Das Matachines
- Desolas
- Durrumbes
- La Penca
- Leyeydas

- Lumenta
- Machetazo
- Metitche
- Pal'alma
- Reyes y Cobardes
- Wild Shot

Zacatecas

Just south of the Chihuahua Desert, in north-central Mexico, lies Zacatecas. The state has an average elevation of 7,316 feet (2,230 meters). Most of it lies within the Sierra Madre Occidental mountains, rising as high as Pico de Teyra at 9,154 ft (2,790 m) above sea level. In fact the capital city, also named Zacatecas, is at an elevation of 8,010 feet (2441 meters) and receives a bit of snow nearly every year. This mountainous land is craggy, punctured by deep valleys and nearly devoid of rivers. Monsoon rains periodically flood stream beds, but their alluvial floors are quickly bereft of the thundering water and covered with nothing but thirsty cracks and dry gravel. Zacatecas features an arid to semiarid climate and very settled weather (Wine Searcher Editorial, 2021). At first glance, it's an inhospitable place for agriculture. A second look reveals thriving mesquite and colorful cacti, fodder for cattle, bean cultivation, and in this tapestry of vibrant desert flora, the pointed leaves of the proud agave that happily populates the rugged expanse of the Zacatecas wilderness.

To the north of Zacatecas is the state of Coahuila, and at the southeast corner of Coahuila is the capital city of Saltillo. This peaceful desert city is home to the supremely popular *Museo del Desierto* or Museum of the Desert (museodeldesierto.org), where visitors are regaled with a well-curated botanical garden, live animal enclosures, immersive indoor archeological displays, extensive desert maps, and exciting educational exhibits. The museum's pavilion delivers soaring mountain views and includes telescopes with which to study Saltillo and the desert beyond. The dinosaur replicas, child-friendly activities, and on-site dining make this a fantastic choice for a family trip.

Zacatecas distilleries employ production methods similar to those used by tequila makers, but Zacatecas falls outside the official tequila DO and its brands are not allowed to display a tequila label. A fun name for these spirits could be "Mountain Tequila". These mirthful Zacatecas creations start with Blue Weber agave and undergo steam distillation, resulting in a less smoky or mezcal-style flavor. Other Zacatecas mezcals are made in a more traditional manner, faithfully adhering to time-honored techniques resembling those of mezcal-crafting procedures prevalent in other regions. Zacatecas mezcals are smooth and easy to drink, but their high minerality and hint of chalkiness make them a worthy choice for the traveler in search of exoticism.

Zacatecas Mezcal Brands

- Don Ramon
- El Cabron
- El Zacatecano
- Hacienda de Banuelos
- Huitzila
- Kimo Sabe
- Luminar
- Mexicat
- Miel de Tierra
- Tierra Adentro
- Tomas
- Vinicola El Consuelo

REGIONAL VARIATIONS IN MEZCAL

You don't have to travel far in Mexico—or even taste different brands of mezcal made in the same places—to realize that not all mezcals are similar. This is as true of mezcal as it is of wine. Each bottle (label and year) has subtle highlights and characteristics in flavor, aroma, and texture. This is because mezcaleros tap into centuries of inherited knowledge to create their own particular nuances of mezcal. Even when they use the same agaves as their closest neighbors or locate down the road or across a valley from another, producers create spirits that are surprisingly exclusive to their palenques. Slight variations in terroir or cultivation decisions may matter less than production choices inspired by generational secrets or an abundance of personal experience. For the consumer, the bewildering alternatives are an endless source of tasting challenge and delight.

Mezcaleros must opt for an indoor or outdoor pit; they must decide whether to line this pit with bricks or local rocks; whether to ferment the nectar in wooden vats, cowhide, or the clay pots their great-grandfather left for them. They must choose between a copper still or the handcrafted replica of the Filipino still someone's ancestors brought to Mexico. They may elect to add a commercial yeast rather than fully put their trust in the individual characteristics of a wild variety or, if in the desert, they might need to add pulque to encourage fermentation. Their water source might come from beneath a tumbling waterfall and be highly oxygenated with faint hints of moss, or it may be drawn from the earth, where it picks up the tang of minerals and salts. They might also add a certain flavoring during the last phase of distillation to create more than one variety of joven mezcal.

The basic process might essentially be the same in a given area, but gradations so tiny as to appear almost insignificant make each mezcal brand and batch slightly different from the next. This is why a mezcal made in one Oaxacan village differs significantly in taste from one made in the next. In the same way, the flavors imbued in a mezcal from the high sierras of Zacatecas vary considerably from those found in a bottle originating at the edges of the northern deserts, while one distilled at the coast has flavors we perceive as maritime compared to those that were forged on the fringes of a native forest.

The Terroir of Mezcal

The concept of terroir was first applied to wine, for which it is well-known, and refers to the natural environment of a particular region and the peculiar characteristics it imparts to its products. Wines from a given terroir have exclusive attributes that are consistent from year to year and are not solely due to a winemaker's expertise. The concept now applies to other foods and beverages, ranging from coffee and chocolate to cheese and meat. Besides being an indicator of where a food or beverage is produced, terroir reflects elements such as the local climate, geography, altitude, and similar factors. When it comes to spirits, the definition of terroir also includes fermentation yeasts, added flavorings and additives, production practices, and aging. They all influence the final product, as summarized below (Vasquez, 2021):

- natural elements—local climate, with its temperature variations, rainfall patterns, precipitation amounts, and winds
- soils—types and composition, pH levels, fertility, and presence of microorganisms
- location—altitude, slope, and proximity to the coast
- environment—botanical diversity, bats, insects, birds, and wildlife

- raw materials—agave species, varieties, and maturation time
- production processes—inherited knowledge and skills, equipment used, and wild or commercial yeasts
- culture—history and local conditions
- human element—choices made by producers

GROWTH OF THE MEZCAL INDUSTRY

Suddenly, everybody wants to drink mezcal, tequila's country cousin that's abruptly gone mainstream—whether it's consumed in its native Mexico or a trendy bar in a large, cosmopolitan city like New York, Madrid, London, Paris, Amsterdam, Tokyo, or Bogotá. In 2020, 66% of DO-certified mezcal was exported internationally, mostly to the United States, and also to over seventy other countries. That year, production surged to 7.85 million liters (2 million gallons) (Arellano-Plaza et al., 2022). Sales by volume in the United States increased by almost 25% in 2019 and a further 14.5% in 2020, and it's anticipated that volumes will grow by an average of 10.5% a year to 2025. As a whole, the sales value of agave spirits grew by around 30.1% or $1.2 billion between 2020 and 2021 (Emen, 2022). Industry players are jockeying for position, with producers and brands amalgamating, expanding, increasing their portfolios, and raising funds for investment. However you look at it, interest in agave spirits is booming and indications are that the trend is set to continue.

With mezcal and other agave spirits set to take the world by storm, there's a proverbial elephant in the room. Mezcal remains very much an artisanal product—from the way it's harvested to production methods that have deep roots in the culture, tradition, family, and ancient inheritance. There are countless ways to make mezcal and so many variables, that scaling up production while maintaining unique aromas and taste experiences is a formidable task.

One of the particular challenges of the boom is the potential supply bottleneck brought about by the length of time most agave species take to mature. Let's not forget that it takes them a long time to reach harvest. Plants such as barley, sugar, or corn are ready in a single season and grapevines typically start yielding their fruit three years after they are planted and faithfully continue to do so for decades and, in some cases, for more than a century. Most agaves take nearly a decade—or two or three—to reach maturity. Producers have to wait seven years after planting before they can harvest the espadin that's used to create around 75% of mezcals, for example (Emen, 2022).

Successful growers are equal to the challenge. They schedule their harvest after the flower spike has bloomed, thus enabling the plant to reproduce naturally. Many also plant more agaves than they use. Mezcaleros understand the true value of these native species, and want to ensure that they will continue to be available for generations to come. Their own business profit and community prosperity also depend on the plant's success. For the same reasons, private landowners also take steps to secure the plant's long-term future.

On public lands, the situation is not so simple. The increasing scarcity of certain wild agave species, particularly around Oaxaca and Puebla, well illustrates the *Tragedy of the Commons*.

An example of this is the tiny village of Santa María Ixcatlán, where mezcal production has declined. Town palenques are running dry of liquor and people. Some agave species have been designated as vulnerable by the International Union for the Conservation of Nature (IUCN). Fortunately, as the number of wild agaves have diminished, due in part to mismanagement, agave plantations have flourished.

Mexican scientists are studying several regions across Mexico to determine how demand for mezcal is impacting agaves and the environment at large. At San Juan Raya, they've initiated a research project that they hope will provide a model for sustainable agave cultivation that will be beneficial to the land and its valuable ecosystem. Around forty-five thousand agaves have been grown from seed in local communities, and these have generated the project's seedlings. When the plants are three years old, they are transplanted near other plants and agave species (Rojo, 2023).

The researchers found that, when planted among other complementary native plants, agaves are more likely to survive. Leguminous shrubs, such as mimosa that fixes nitrogen in its roots, are particularly beneficial when planted in association with agaves. A third of the plants will be left in these plantations to provide food for bats and other animals that rely on the pollen and nectar from agave flowers. Participating communities will receive the rest for mezcal production. Similar projects are being rolled out in other areas, including Oaxaca (Rojo, 2023).

While some Mexican states have passed laws to protect the genetic integrity of agaves, mezcal producers themselves have also sought solutions to maintain their ecosystems in the face of skyrocketing demand for mezcal. The researchers hope that their efforts, supported by Mexican environmental authorities and local growers, will enable them to offer a management plan guiding the cultivation and use of agave for mezcal production.

Diversity is the very essence of mezcal and part of its charm. Yet, in the rush to meet ever-expanding demand, the industry risks relying on fields of genetically similar espadin that can potentially be wiped out by the proliferation of a single pest or disease. Not only that, but turning mezcal homogenous also undermines its artisanal nature, the very thing that drives its popularity.

Scaling up mezcal production is a complex task due to the drink's handcrafted nature and the countless variables involved. One solution is to facilitate an increase in the number of small producers, thereby creating more economic and employment opportunities. At the same time, some brands that are unable to add more products to their inventory are considering partnering with other producers. This can be an excellent option for small outfits that may discover strength in numbers. A major difficulty across the industry is that big, international players acting as intermediaries tend to reap most of the benefits, while those actually making mezcal see very little of those funds. To address this issue, some brands have chosen not to outsource their production, ensuring that their partners receive sufficient financial compensation.

Another difficulty is that the DO certification has become more demanding. Its administrators no longer merely allow producers to use the name *mezcal* on their labels. They have begun specifying certain production methods and standards that certified producers need to adhere to. Fortunately or unfortunately, depending on one's perspective, this will inevitably lead to some industrialization and further modernization. Producers are already using solar power to run mechanized tahonas, for example. Some brands have reduced their artisanal approach as they focus on improving their efficiency and reducing costs. The new regulations lead to greater involvement by big corporations with funds to buy up large quantities of agave, raising prices and negatively impacting smaller operations.

While some cheer the advent of industrialization, others bemoan its potential to undermine the artisanal, handcrafted nature of mezcal. The sheer size of the mezcal region is to its advantage, however, as it creates scope for newcomers. There are still plenty of opportunities to develop and market new mezcal brands in and beyond Oaxaca. Some producers source products from several states within the mezcal DO region. While there are challenges, resourceful mezcal makers will likely be able to scale up their operations while retaining their product's reputation as a unique, handcrafted Mexican spirit.

As you have seen in this chapter, mezcal has long been part of the culture and traditions of many regions of Mexico. The strong Mexican sun, that once shone bright over Nahuatl-speaking villages or modest Filipino stills, now illuminates authentic mom-and-pop operations and creative young businesses alike. Each person brings expertise to the table; each brand functions within the dictates of its area; each agave plant can translate into a successful endeavor.

The increasing demand for mezcal is bringing a suite of challenges and opportunities that producers and authorities will need to navigate in the coming years. In the meantime, the mezcal public around the globe can celebrate the survival of ancestral spirits and the arrival of new labels. The growing availability and exciting interpretations of this vivacious spirit are sure to bring life to your large gathering and personal enjoyment to your private moment.

You are alone at last after a very long day. The evening shadows are lengthening outside. Your palate is still bitter at the memory of the takeout rations you tolerated over lunch. You grab the mezcal copita and cautiously release a single drop onto your outer forearm. You bring it to your nose and inhale. The sensation hits you strongly at first, shattering your gustatory boredom as with a hammer. After a moment, the finer aromatics meld with the natural oils in your skin to reassure you and redefine your feeling of weekday fatigue. The smell is soft and comforting, and only yours to enjoy. You exhale. After a few moments, you take your first micro-sip. It tickles the roof of your mouth and you smile, although no one is looking. You notice the ticking of the analog clock on the wall and hear the faint echoes of children playing in the distance. Suddenly, you feel cool as the evening breeze brushes your face and greets the warmth now emanating from your core. This is the feeling of balance, and of noticing the fine details which you were heretofore too preoccupied to even register.

Perhaps you do not wish to drink (even micro-sips) alone. If so, your private moment can easily become a private event; you need only share with another the exquisite elixir in your prized bottle. When life calls for a larger celebration, one or more bottles of mezcal may be all you need to transform an ordinary day into a memorable occasion.

Need to launch a product, revive a dispirited office, or enjoy a special reunion? Mezcal will ignite the crowd's enthusiasm and a fine cook or caterer will create the perfect dishes to make your moment a great success. Like fine wine, mezcal can be paired with a range of delicious foods. You'll discover more about the gastronomic aspects of mezcal, together with some great recipes to try, in the next chapter.

Saludos a Sinaloa a Chihuahua y a Durango
Para todos mis respetos
Lo que les digo es muy cierto
No me gustan los problemas
Yo no soy hombre de pleito
Tengo amigos de montones
Porque soy hombre derecho
Como lo dije al principio
Soy el amo del desierto

Greetings to Sinaloa, Chihuahua, and Durango
With all my respect
What I tell you is very sure I don't like problems
I am not a man of litigation
I have tons of friends
Because I am a man of integrity
As I said at the beginning
I am the master of the desert

- El Bandolero Meño Sanchez, "El Amo Del Desierto"
-The Highwayman Meño Sanchez, "The Master of the Desert"

PAIRING MEZCAL WITH OAXACAN CUISINE

> *Oaxaca is a little bit of mischief, a little bit of improvisation.*
>
> — FAUSTO ZAPATA

> *Oaxaca is at the heart of mole country, a triangle along with Puebla and Veracruz that defines the most complex Mexican cooking.*
>
> — RICK BAYLESS

This chapter provides a quick guide to pairing mezcal with Oaxacan cuisine. Awaken your culinary creativity and find new ways to enjoy and explore mezcal's unique flavor profiles.

THE ART OF PAIRING MEZCAL WITH FOOD

You're probably familiar with food and wine pairings—or even with pairing cocktails with food. You might be wondering whether

it's possible to pair food with spirits. It is certainly more challenging, as the high alcohol content of spirits, together with their
flavors and the sensation of heat generated by them, can overwhelm certain foods. The good news, however, is that it's not
impossible.

Spirits, especially drinks like mezcal, have complex flavors that
complement the taste of certain foods. Vodka is a good example of
this. It is often consumed with appetizers, called *zakuski* in Russia,
that are expressly prepared to be enjoyed with the drink. The
smokiness of bourbon, for example, goes well with grilled food at
a barbecue—and this could apply to smokier mezcals, too. Gin has
citrusy, spicy flavors that act almost like seasoning when paired
with foods like salmon. Some mezcals have similar flavor profiles
and could fulfill the same role.

Tickle Your Taste Buds

Here are a few taste sensations that work well with mezcal (The Best Mezcal, n.d.):

- If you're drinking a high-quality, smoky mezcal, consider pairing it with bitter, slightly smoky foods like mole, complex sauces made with bitter, leafy greens like spinach and kale, or even something as simple as red chilies scattered over avocado on toast.
- Mezcal complements salty foods—and especially appetizers—very well.
- Lighter, sweeter mezcals combine well with desserts and sweet foods, especially caramel and bitter chocolate—or tropical fruits if you don't have much of a sweet tooth.
- Smoked meats, cheeses, and even vegetables combine well with the smokiness of mezcal.
- Mezcals go well with anything that has salty or earthy flavors. Try it with foods flavored with garlic, pepper, chilies, rosemary, thyme, or cinnamon. It will bring out the other flavors, and they in turn will enhance the complexity of the mezcal.

Chef's Choice

Chefs recommend that mezcal be paired with the following cuisines (Sweitzer-Lammé, 2022):

- *Goan* cuisine, which tends to be smoky and spicy, particularly when served with curries flavored with hand-ground spices and coconut vinegar
- cheese plates used as a starter or appetizer before a meal

that will include delicacies like fresh gooseberries, pickled wild mustard seeds, and honey on the comb

- desserts based on coconut and vanilla
- tomato salads containing herbs like basil, together with olive oil and fresh orange
- spicy foods and Mexican appetizers like guacamole
- roasted chicken with mushrooms and goji berries
- pork with crackling
- fish and seafood

MEZCAL PAIRINGS IN OAXACA

How do Oaxacans enjoy mezcal? As you would expect, food pairings assembled in the places where these spirits are produced and consumed bring out the best of both. They're part of the fine tradition of mezcal-making and its alliance with Mexican culture. Like many other alcoholic beverages, mezcal is often served with snacks that help to pad the stomach while showcasing the flavors of the spirit. I suggest that you enjoy smokier mezcals in the latter part of your meal as the smoky sensation can linger on your palate.

Below are some common pairings when mezcal is savored in Mexico (Lampert, 2023):

- Sal de gusano, as mentioned previously, is often consumed with mezcal. This finely ground seasoning combines the flavors of sea salt, chilies and dried agave worm. Its rich taste sensations complement virtually any type of mezcal. The practice of dusting it on orange slices, which are eaten while mezcal is sipped, helps bring out all those amazing flavors.
- You might have heard rumors about the new trend of eating insects as a protein source. The Oaxacans are ahead

of the game, as their *chapulín* snacks consist of toasted, seasoned grasshoppers. Flavored with chiles and a range of salts, they have flavors and textures that intensify the earthy and fruity flavors of most mezcals.

- Almost any cheese can be enjoyed with mezcal. In Oaxaca, as well as in the dairy farming regions of central and northern Mexico, this cheese is likely to be *quesillo*. Cheeses heighten the creamy, lactic notes of some mezcals.
- A coffee-chocolate cake, not-so-mysteriously called *chocolate y café*, is a perfect selection to be enjoyed with mezcal, and it's a firm favorite in Oaxaca. You can easily savor either chocolate or coffee treats with mezcal. They touch off a delicious taste sensation at the moment of impact.
- Pairing rich, traditional sauces like mole with mezcal might sound like overkill, but it works. The intense flavors of the mole rise to match those of mezcal, so they complement one another. I will provide a table of suggested mole and mezcal pairings later in this chapter.
- Peanuts are found in most bars and Mexico's mezcalerias are no exception. Their take on peanuts is a little different from what you may have noticed elsewhere. Served skin-on, drizzled in a little olive oil and lime, and seasoned with garlic and chili, they are the perfect accompaniment to mezcal.
- The sweetness of sliced chunks of melon and mango sprinkled with traditional tajín spice (a combination of chili peppers, salt, and dehydrated lime) takes the edge off the mezcal and cools down the alcohol burn.
- Rose-colored agua de Jamaica is a Caribbean *fresca* made from steeped hibiscus buds, sugar, and chilies. Refreshingly different, it's often enjoyed alongside mezcal to counter the spirit's burning sensation.

CRAFTING MEZCAL-INFUSED CULINARY CREATIONS

In this section, you'll find recipes inspired by mezcal and Oaxacan cuisine. Enjoy!

Oysters Oaxacafeller

Prep Time: 45 mins

Cook Time: 25 mins

Total Time: 70 mins

Yield: Enough for 24 oysters

Nutritional Information per Serving:

Total Calories	Carbohydrates	Fat	Protein
75	5 g	4 g	5 g

Ingredients:

- 24 fresh oysters
- 2 medium-sized (6 1/4 oz; 180 g) poblano peppers
- 4 large (1 oz; 28 g) scallions
- 2 large (4 oz; 113 g) shallots
- 1/2 cup Mexican crema or sour cream or crème fraîche
- 2 medium cloves garlic
- 1/2 bunch (1 1/2 cups) fresh cilantro—tender stems and leaves
- 1/2 cup panko breadcrumbs
- 1/8 tsp ground coriander
- vegetable cooking spray
- 2 tbsp unsalted butter
- kosher salt

- rock (ice cream) salt
- cayenne pepper
- finely grated zest of 1 lime
- 1 tbsp mezcal (optional)
- lime wedges (for serving)

Directions:

1. Stem the peppers, halve them lengthwise, and remove the seeds. Thinly slice the shallots and garlic cloves. Roughly chop the cilantro. Scrub the oysters.
2. Move the oven rack so that it is 6 in. (15 cm) below the broiler and preheat it on high. While you wait for it to heat up, line a baking sheet with foil and spray it with vegetable cooking spray. Lightly coat the skins of the peppers and scallions with the oil as well.
3. Place them on the baking sheet (the peppers should be cut-side down).
4. Cook the vegetables for 5–8 minutes, until they are soft and slightly browned.
5. Place the scallions on a cutting board and set aside.
6. Move the peppers to the center of the baking tray and gather up the edges of the tin foil to make a pouch.
7. Steam them until their skins separate easily from the flesh. Carefully peel off and discard the skins. Chop the scallions and poblanos into 1/2 in. (1 cm) thick pieces.
8. Heat the butter in a medium saucepan on medium heat until it starts foaming. Add the shallots and a generous pinch of salt. Cook and stir lightly for about 6–8 minutes, until softened. Add the poblanos and scallions and cook until the vegetables have released all their liquid. Continue cooking until that has evaporated, which should take another 3–5 minutes.

9. Stir in the crema, ground coriander, and lime zest. Cook for another minute, until everything is well combined and the mixture has thickened.

10. Remove the saucepan from the heat and add the mezcal (if using).

11. Transfer the mixture to a food processor bowl and process for 30 seconds. Pause to scrape down the bowl as needed. You should end up with a coarse paste.

12. Add the cilantro and continue processing until it is thoroughly mixed into the paste.

13. Add the bread crumbs and pulse until everything is well combined.

14. Season lightly with salt.

15. Transfer the mixture to a small pastry bag. Alternatively, spoon it into a small mixing bowl and cover it with plastic wrap so that the wrap adheres to the mixture.

16. You can make the paste the day before and store it in the refrigerator. Allow it to return to room temperature before serving.

17. Adjust the oven rack again so that it is 6 in. (15 cm) below the grill and preheat the broiler on high. Line the baking sheet with 1/2 in. (1 cm) of rock salt, ensuring that it is evenly spread.

18. Shuck the oysters and lay them on the baking sheet. Pipe or spoon the mixture over the oysters, ensuring that each one is completely covered. Using a butter knife, smooth the paste.

19. Broil the oysters for 4–6 minutes, until the topping starts to brown and the oysters are warmed through. Check on them frequently. Remove them from the oven when done and season them lightly with cayenne.

20. Serve them immediately with lime wedges and mezcal at the table.

Mexican Fish Ceviche (Ceviche de Pescado)

Prep Time: 10 mins

Cook Time: 30 mins

Total Time: 40 mins

Yield: 4 servings

Nutritional Information per Serving:

Total Calories	Carbohydrates	Fat	Protein
216	12 g	9 g	23 g

Ingredients:

- 16 oz (1 lb; 450 g) fresh, firm white fish (halibut, sea bass or snapper)
- 2 Roma tomatoes
- 1 cucumber
- 1 avocado
- 1/2 red onion
- 1 jalapeño pepper
- 1/2 bunch cilantro
- 1 tsp kosher salt
- juice of 5–6 limes (about 1/2 cup)
- juice of 1 lemon (about 3 tsp)
- 1 tsp mezcal (optional)

Chef's Notes:

- You can use several white fish for this recipe besides the ones listed above (Mexicans traditionally use sea bass). Try cod, mahi mahi, tuna, or marlin. You can also use shellfish like shrimp, crabs, scallops, or squid. Make sure the fish is the freshest and best quality you can obtain, preferably fresh-caught from a local fish market.
- Marinating time varies from 30 minutes to 4 hours, depending on how tender you want the fish. As a rough guide, marinating the fish for 30 minutes will tenderize it and it will turn opaque, although it should not look raw. After an hour, the fish will also be opaque—this is equivalent to medium-cooked meat. After 4 hours, the fish will start to toughen and may lose some flavor.

Directions:

1. Purchase deboned fish. Skin it, dice it into small pieces, and place it in a non-reactive glass or porcelain bowl.
2. Add the lime and lemon juice and the mezcal, and stir in the fish.
3. Cover the bowl with plastic wrap and let it marinate in the refrigerator for 30 minutes to 4 hours (see notes above). The fish will turn opaque as the citrus juices do their work.
4. While the fish is marinating, prepare the vegetables. Peel and chop the onion. Peel and dice the cucumber. Dice the tomatoes. Remove the skin and pit from the avocado and dice it. Seed and dice the jalapeño pepper. Chop the cilantro.
5. Combine the vegetables in a large glass bowl. Add the salt and stir it in.

6. When the fish has finished marinating to your satisfaction, remove it from the refrigerator. Don't drain it.
7. Add the vegetables and stir gently to combine.
8. Check the flavor and add more salt to taste, if needed.
9. Serve in glasses or on a plate with tortilla chips.

Shrimp Mezcal

This recipe is similar to ceviche but uses mezcal as an ingredient.

Prep Time: 15 mins

Cook Time: 8 mins

Total Time: 23 mins

Yield: 4 servings

Nutritional Information per Serving:

Total Calories	Carbohydrates	Fat	Protein
302	10 g	21 g	18 g

Ingredients:

- 16 oz (450 g) shrimp
- 1 medium ripe avocado
- 2 medium tomatoes
- 1 oz (30 ml) mezcal
- 1 tsp garlic, minced
- 1/4 cup fresh cilantro
- 1/4 cup butter
- 1 tsp green Tabasco sauce
- juice of 1 medium lime

Directions:

1. Peel and devein the shrimp.
2. Peel and dice the avocado and chop the tomatoes and cilantro.
3. For 1 min, sauté the shrimp in a large, stainless steel skillet (don't use a non-stick pan).
4. Add the garlic and mezcal and light it with a match.
5. Add the rest of the ingredients except for the cilantro and tomatoes as the flame burns down.
6. Simmer for 3 minutes, or until the salmon turns pink.
7. Serve immediately. Garnish with the tomatoes and cilantro.

Oaxacan Drunken Salsa (Salsa Borracha de Oaxaca)

Prep Time: 10 mins

Cook Time: 15 mins

Total Time: 25 mins

Yield: 2 cups

Nutritional Information per Serving:

Total Calories	Carbohydrates	Fat	Protein
154	17 g	2 g	2 g

Ingredients:

- 12 oz (340 g) tomatillos
- 4 whole chipotle chilies in adobo
- 1 medium white onion
- 2 garlic cloves (do not peel)

- 1 tsp sugar
- 1 tsp salt
- 4 tbsp mezcal

Chef's Note:

- You can use canned tomatillos for this recipe. Be sure to drain them before using.

Directions:

1. Cut the onion into 1/2 in. (1 cm) thick slices. If using canned tomatillos, drain them. Rinse off the chilies and set aside.
2. Place a heavy skillet on medium heat and roast the tomatillos (if using fresh) together with the onion and garlic. When the vegetables start charring, turn them and roast the other side.
3. Remove the pan from the heat when everything is charred. Peel the garlic.
4. Place the chipotle chilies, roasted or canned tomatillos, charred garlic and onion, salt, and sugar in a blender. Blend until the mixture is very smooth.
5. Scrape into a bowl and stir in the mezcal.
6. Serve immediately or refrigerate for later consumption.

Salmon With Mezcal

Prep Time: 5 mins

Cook Time: 6 mins

Total Time: 11 mins

Yield: 4 servings

Nutritional Information per Serving:

Total Calories	Carbohydrates	Fat	Protein
175	0 g	10.5 g	18.8 g

Ingredients:

- 1 salmon filet
- butter and olive oil (1 tbsp of each)
- 2 oz (60 ml) mezcal
- 3 tbsp Santa Cruz chili pepper
- 2 tbsp ground black pepper
- lemon slices (for serving)

Directions:

1. In a large pan, melt the olive oil and butter.
2. As the mixture melts, dip a pastry brush into it and lightly coat both sides of the salmon.
3. Top the filet with the chili powder and ground black pepper and smooth it with your fingers to make a crust.
4. When the pan is hot, place the salmon in it, crust side down. Cook for 3 minutes.
5. Flip the salmon onto its other side and cook until it is cooked, about 3 more minutes.
6. Pour the mezcal over the salmon and heat through.
7. Serve with the lemon slices.

Lamb Barbacoa

Prep Time: 1 hour, 15 mins

Cook Time: 5 hours

Resting Time: 4 hours

Total Time: 10 hours, 15 mins

Yield: 8 servings

Nutritional Information per Serving:

Total Calories	Carbohydrates	Fat	Protein
275	12 g	11 g	21 g

Ingredients:

Marinade:

- 1 tbsp ground cumin
- 1 tbsp smoked paprika
- 2 tsp black peppercorns
- 2 tsp whole coriander seeds
- 1 tsp ground cinnamon
- 1 tbsp onion powder
- 2 tsp dried oregano
- 2 tbsp kosher salt
- 1 tbsp fresh habanero or pequin chili peppers, sliced
- 6 garlic cloves
- 2 tbsp ground mustard
- 2 tbsp raw honey
- 2 tbsp avocado oil, lard, or mild vegetable oil
- 1/4 cup mezcal

Lamb:

- 64 oz (4 lb; 1.8 kg) bone-in lamb pieces (shank, neck, or leg)
- 2 large, white onions, thinly sliced
- 2 tbsp avocado oil, lard, or mild vegetable oil
- 1/2 cup mezcal
- water

Directions:

1. Begin by making the marinade.
2. Place the peppercorns, paprika, cumin, coriander seeds, cinnamon, onion powder, oregano, and salt into a spice grinder, mini food processor, or pestle and mortar. Grind them for 10–15 seconds, until the oils release and the mixture becomes fragrant.
3. Add the sliced chilies (or peppers) and garlic. Grind them together with the spices for 1 minute, until a chalky paste forms.
4. Scrape the paste into a large bowl with a wooden spoon. Add the rest of the ingredients and whisk until everything is thoroughly combined.
5. Put on disposable gloves before continuing with the next step, as chilies can irritate the skin.
6. Add the lamb to the marinade. If the bowl is too small, you can put the lamb on a large baking sheet. Rub the marinade all over the meat using your hands, being careful to include any fissures in the meat.
7. Place the lamb in the refrigerator. It should rest for at least 4 hours or overnight if possible.
8. When you are ready to cook the lamb, remove it from the refrigerator and allow it to warm up to room temperature.

9. Preheat the oven to 275 °F (135 °C).

10. Open the window or turn on your ventilation system, as chilies in the marinade may release particles or cause discomfort.

11. Warm the oil in a large, ovenproof stockpot over medium-high heat. Brown the meat on all sides, working in batches. This will take about 10–14 minutes.

12. Transfer all the browned meat to a baking sheet or large plate.

13. Reduce the heat to medium. Cook the sliced onions for 7–10 minutes until brown and caramelized.

14. Pour the mezcal onto the onions and scrape any bits off the bottom of the pot. Remove the pot from the heat after the liquid has evaporated slightly.

15. Return the lamb to the pot. Add 2–3 cups of water so that the pot is half-full. Cover and place in the oven.

16. Roast for 4–5 hours until the lamb is tender and falling off the bone. Remove it from the oven and let it cool for at least 30 minutes.

17. Transfer it to a roasting pan and pull the meat off the bones. Discard any fat or gristle. Skim the fat off the braising liquid.

18. If you are serving the barbacoa for tacos or with rice, add the meat to the pot with the braising liquid and onions, and heat it over low heat as needed.

19. If you plan to serve the barbacoa as carnitas, slide the meat pan beneath the broiler to crisp the edges. Turn it as needed.

Smoky Queso Fundido Borracho

Prep Time: 15 mins

Cook Time: 10 mins

Total Time: 25 mins

Yield: 6 servings

Nutritional Information per Serving:

Total Calories	Carbohydrates	Fat	Protein
262	3 g	20 g	17 g

Ingredients:

- 4 oz (115 g) ground chorizo sausage, cooked
- 1 lb (16 oz; 450 g) Mexican Oaxaca (Asadero) or Monterey Jack cheese
- 1 poblano chili
- 1 large jalapeño pepper
- 1 large, ripe tomato
- 1 medium onion, diced (enough to make 1 cup)
- 1/2 tsp kosher salt
- 1 tsp fresh cilantro
- 2 oz (60 ml) top-shelf mezcal or blanco tequila
- juice of 1 lime
- warm tortillas, tortilla chips, or pork rinds (for serving)

Directions:

1. Roast the poblano by holding it over a gas burner with tongs. Turn the pepper as you do this, so it will be lightly

charred on all sides. Alternatively, you can do this over a grill or beneath a broiler.

2. Place the roasted poblano in a bowl covered with plastic wrap and allow it to steam for 10 minutes.

3. Cut it in half and remove the stem and seeds. Gently scrape off the charred pieces but do not rinse the pepper. Dice and set aside.

4. Cut the cheese into cubes. Dice the onion, mince the cilantro, and seed and dice the tomato. If you prefer, you can leave the tomato seeds.

5. Over medium-high heat, warm a cast-iron skillet. Sauté the chorizo and onions for 5–6 minutes, breaking up the sausage as it cooks.

6. Remove from the heat and add the diced poblano, jalapeño, salt, mezcal (or tequila) and lime juice. Return to medium-high heat. Cook for another 3 minutes, stirring often, until the liquid has largely evaporated.

7. Turn down the heat to low. Add the cheese cubes. Cook, stirring the mixture often, until the cheese is melted, and then stir in the cilantro.

8. Serve hot with warm tortillas, tortilla chips, or pork rinds.

Mole Negro

Prep Time: 40 mins

Cook Time: 2 hours, 15 mins

Total Time: 2 hours, 55 mins

Yield: 4–6 servings (chicken) and 5 cups mole sauce

Nutritional Information per Serving:

Total Calories	Carbohydrates	Fat	Protein
976	66 g	65 g	41 g

Ingredients:

Mole Sauce:

- 2 medium tomatoes (8 oz; 1/2 lb; 226 g)
- 2 medium tomatillos (4 oz; 1/4 lb; 113 g)
- 1/2 onion, unpeeled
- 2 garlic heads, whole and unpeeled
- 1/4 cup walnuts
- 7 almonds
- 1 cinnamon stick
- 1/8 piece whole nutmeg
- 3 whole cloves
- 2 allspice berries
- 1/2 in. pc fresh ginger root or 1/2 tsp ground ginger
- 1/3 cup sesame seeds (plus more for garnish)
- 1/4 cup raisins
- 2 bay leaves
- 2 avocado leaves
- 1 tbsp dried oregano
- 2 tsp dried thyme
- 8 guajillo chilies
- 4 mulato chili peppers or ancho negro
- 4 dry chilhuacle chili peppers or cascabel chilies
- 4 cups chicken stock, divided (plus extra for thinning)
- 1 tsp mezcal (optional)
- 3 tbsp oil or lard
- 3/4 cup (6 oz; 170 g) Mexican chocolate

- 1/3 cup granulated sugar
- 1 bolillo
- 1 tbsp kosher salt (more to taste, if needed)

Chicken

- 6 chicken thighs (bone-in and skin-on)
- 1/4 cup water
- 12 garlic cloves
- 1 tbsp kosher salt (more to taste)
- rice and warm tortillas (for serving)

Directions:

Chef's Notes:

- This recipe is based on the traditional Oaxacan method of making mole, where the toasted ingredients are prepared outside using a *comal* (traditional griddle) atop an open wood fire. The chilies are normally charred over the fire—this creates a smoky, ashy flavor—together with the onion, garlic cloves, tomatoes and tomatillos.
- The mole sauce can be made up to a week ahead of time and kept covered in the refrigerator, which improves the flavors. Reheat when you are ready to use it. You can add a little chicken broth if it becomes too thick.

Making the Mole:

1. Chop the chocolate and set aside.
2. Cut the bolillo in half and toast it. Set aside.
3. Seed and stem the chilies. On medium heat on a flat griddle or comal, toast them, stirring them around until

they release their aromas and turn darker. Then, remove them from the griddle and set aside.

4. Toast the sesame seeds until they begin to pop. Set aside.
5. Toast the raisins for 2 minutes, until they swell and start darkening, and set aside.
6. Toast all the spices and nuts in one go, moving them around on the griddle. Once they start releasing their aromas, remove them from the heat and set aside.
7. Briefly toast the bay leaves, avocado leaves, thyme, and oregano on the griddle for about 5–10 seconds, until they start releasing their aromas, and set aside.
8. Turn on the ventilation hood over your stove and set it to high. For gas stoves, remove the grate and turn the flame on low. Place the unpeeled onion and garlic directly on the plate or flame to cook for about 20 minutes, turning frequently, until the outside turns black (the garlic cloves should be soft enough to slide out of their skins). Set aside, cool, and peel off the skins.
9. Do the same with the tomatoes and tomatillos. Turn them so that all surfaces are charred. This takes about 10 minutes. You need not peel them.
10. Place the toasted chilies on a high-sided comal or use a large frying pan. Ensure that it is big enough to hold the water you will be adding. Place the pan on high heat and toast the chilies until they are completely blackened and very dry. If you are doing this in your kitchen, keep the ventilation hood turned up high and open all windows and doors. You might want to wear a face mask to protect your face from the smoke, as well as any tiny flecks that might come off the chilies as you do this.
11. Turn off the heat if you are using a stove. Carefully remove the pan from the stovetop or the fire. (If you are working in your kitchen, take the pan outside.) Set it on a non-

flammable surface like a concrete slab, on top of a grill, or somewhere similar. Make sure the space around it is clear of any flammable debris or items. Ensure that you have a pitcher of hot water close by.

12. Set the chilies on fire using a kitchen torch, gas fire lighter, or something similar. Allow them to burn down to their carbonized shells. This takes about 1–2 min. It's a very smoky process, and the fire is intense. Carefully pour the hot water over the burnt chilies to extinguish the flames. Let them rest in the water for 5 minutes to soften and then pour it out, being careful to retain the chilies.

13. Return to the kitchen. Mix the softened chilies with the toasted ingredients previously prepared.

14. Measure out 1 1/2 cups of the chicken broth and blend the ingredients in a high-powered blender. You may need to work in batches. Ensure that the paste produced is very smooth.

15. Place a large pot or Dutch oven over medium-high heat. Add the lard or oil and allow it to become very hot.

16. Add the chili mixture to the pot and stir frequently for approximately 10 minutes until it thickens.

17. Add 2 cups of chicken broth to the mixture, together with the bay and avocado leaves, chocolate, mezcal, sugar, and salt. Bring to a boil and stir for 5 minutes, until the chocolate has melted.

18. Blend the toasted bread with 1/2 cup chicken broth. Add this to the chili and chocolate mixture, cover, and turn the heat down to a very low setting. Allow the mixture to simmer and thicken while you prepare the chicken. Check it regularly to ensure that it is not burning and sticking to the bottom.

Preparing the Chicken:

1. Start by making a garlic paste. To do this, grind the garlic and salt together using a mortar and pestle (*molcajete*). Add 1/4 cup water and combine thoroughly to produce a smooth paste. You can also use a blender to make the paste.
2. Place the mixture in a skillet large enough to hold all the chicken pieces in a single layer. Heat it over medium heat until it is simmering.
3. Add the chicken, placing it skin-side down in the skillet. Simmer until the liquid reduces and the chicken releases its liquids and oils. Once the liquid is completely reduced, turn the heat down low.
4. Fry the chicken for about an hour in the remaining mixture until it is completely cooked. Turn the pieces approximately every 10 minutes.
5. Once the chicken is ready, remove the avocado and bay leaves from your mole sauce. Check the taste and add more salt if necessary.
6. Spoon the mole over the individual chicken pieces. Sprinkle with sesame seeds.
7. Serve with rice and warm tortillas. Pair with a Tobalá mezcal.
8. You will very likely have some left-over mole. It can be covered and left in the refrigerator for 7–10 days. It can also be frozen and will keep for up to 6 months.

It is well worth exploring the delightful interactions between mezcals and the colorful palette of Mexican moles. The table below shows some suggested pairings.

Type of Mole	Suggested Mezcal Pairing
Mole Almendrado	Cuixe (made with *Agave rhodacantha*)
Mole Amarillo	Espadin (made with *Agave angustifolia*) Distilled with Chocolate or *Destilado con Cacao*
Mole Chichilo	Espadin
Mole Coloradito	Tepeztate (made with *Agave marmorata*)
Mole Estofado	Madrecuixe (made with *Agave karwinskii*)
Mole Manchamentel	Mexicano (made with *Agave rhodacantha*)
Mole Negro	Tobalá (made with *Agave potatorum*)
Mole Poblano	Tobalá
Mole Rojo	Ancho or Papalote (made with *Agave cupreata*)
Mole Verde	Espadin

Instant Pot Smoky Mezcal Pulled Pork Tacos

Prep Time: 15 mins

Cook Time: 40 mins

Total Time: 55 mins

Yield: 5 servings

Nutritional Information per Serving:

Total Calories	Carbohydrates	Fat	Protein
284	17 g	15 g	19 g

Ingredients:

- 64 oz (4 lb; 1.8 kg) boneless pork rump or shoulder, quartered
- 2 jalapeños
- 2 red bell peppers
- 1 tbsp olive oil
- 1 bay leaf

- 1 tsp each white and black pepper
- 1 tsp coarse salt
- 1 tsp smoked paprika
- 1 tsp cumin
- 1/4 cup mezcal
- 1/2 cup lime juice
- 1 tbsp apple cider vinegar
- 1 cup broth

Salsa:

- 1 tbsp lime juice
- 1 fresh mango, diced
- 1 1/2 cups grape tomatoes
- 1/2 cup fresh cilantro
- 1/4 tsp salt

Serving and Topping Suggestions:

- soft corn tortillas
- queso fresco, crumbled
- avocado, diced

Directions:

1. In a small bowl, mix together the seasonings (white and black pepper, coarse salt, cumin, and paprika).
2. Rub the seasoning over the pork.
3. In the instant pot, pour the olive oil into the insert and select Sauté. Roast the pork for about 4 minutes on each side so it browns evenly.
4. Remove the meat and set it on a plate. Use the mezcal to deglaze the pot insert and scrape up all the browned meat

fragments. Add the lime juice, apple cider vinegar, and broth to the pot and turn off the Sauté function.

5. Thinly slice the bell peppers and jalapeños.
6. Set the trivet at the bottom of the pot. Layer the pork pieces on top. Position the bell peppers and jalapeño closely around the meat.
7. Seal the instant pot. Pressure cook the meat for 35 minutes. Allow the carnitas to vent for 10 minutes, and then manually vent for the rest of the cook time.
8. Heat the oven to 425 °F (220 °C) and line a baking sheet with heavy foil.
9. Prepare the salsa. Halve the grape tomatoes, dice the mango, and chop the cilantro. Mix together with the rest of the ingredients. Set aside.
10. Remove the pork from the pressure cooker when venting is completed, and shred the meat. Return it to the pot and stir, coating the meat with the remaining juices.
11. Transfer the pork to the baking sheet using a slotted spoon or tongs. Bake for 10 minutes. The edges should turn crispy and caramelized.
12. While the pork is baking, toast the tortillas by heating them in a dry pan. Remove the pulled pork from the oven and divide it evenly among the tortillas.
13. Add your favorite toppings.

Any leftover pork can be refrigerated for up to 3 days. Reheat it in the oven on a baking sheet and cook under the broiler for up to 5 minutes.

Mezcal Barbecue Sauce

Prep Time: 10 mins

Cook Time: 30 mins

Total Time: 40 mins

Yield: 4–5 cups

Nutritional Information per Serving:

Total Calories	Carbohydrates	Fat	Protein
488	15.7 g	0.8 g	1.8 g

Ingredients:

- 1 cup apple cider vinegar (add more to taste for extra kick)
- 4 cups ketchup (tomato sauce)
- 1/2 cup mezcal
- 2/3 cup molasses
- 2/3 cup brown sugar
- 2 small yellow onions
- 6 garlic cloves
- 4 tbsp yellow mustard
- 1 tbsp chili powder
- 1 tsp cayenne pepper
- 1 tsp ground black pepper

Directions:

1. Dice the onions and mince the cloves.
2. Melt the butter in a saucepan on medium-high heat.
3. Reduce to medium heat and sauté the onions until

softened. Add the mezcal and cook until the onions are translucent. Add the garlic and sauté for another minute.

4. Add the rest of the ingredients and bring the mixture to a boil before reducing the heat to a medium-high setting again. Simmer for about 20–30 minutes until the sauce thickens.
5. Pour the sauce into a blender and whizz until well combined and smooth.
6. Cool to room temperature before serving.

Mexican Chocolate Cake

Prep Time: 25 mins

Cook Time: 35 mins

Total Time: 1 hour

Yield: 18 servings

Nutritional Information per Serving:

Total Calories	Carbohydrates	Fat	Protein
430	61 g	20 g	3 g

Ingredients:

- 1 cup unsalted butter
- 2 cups granulated sugar
- 2 cups all-purpose flour
- 1 cup unsweetened cocoa powder
- 1–2 tbsp instant espresso powder
- 1 1/4 tsp baking soda
- 1 1/2 tsp cinnamon
- 1/4–1/2 tsp cayenne pepper

- 1/2 tsp salt
- 1 cup semi-sweet chocolate chips (use Mexican chocolate)
- 2 large eggs
- 2 cups water
- 1 tsp vanilla extract
- 1/2 tsp mezcal (optional)

Frosting:

- 1/2 cup unsalted butter (at room temperature)
- 3 cups powdered sugar
- 1 tbsp cinnamon
- 1 tsp vanilla extract
- 2–3 tbsp milk
- pinch salt

Directions:

1. Preheat the oven to 325 ºF (165 °C).
2. Lightly coat a 9 in. x 13 in. (22 cm x 33 cm) baking pan with cooking spray and set aside.
3. Melt the butter in a large saucepan over medium heat. Whisk in the espresso powder and cocoa. After they are fully combined, add the water and sugar. Whisk until everything is well mixed and smooth.
4. Remove from the heat and let the mixture rest for 5 minutes.
5. In a medium bowl, mix together the flour, baking soda, cinnamon, salt, pepper, and chocolate chips. Set aside.
6. Whisk the eggs, vanilla and mezcal (if desired) into the butter-chocolate mixture until well mixed. Gently stir in the flour mixture using a wooden spoon or spatula. Mix by

hand until everything is well combined and the batter is smooth.

7. Pour the batter into the baking pan. Bake for 30–35 minutes, until a toothpick inserted into the center comes out clean.

8. Remove from the oven and cool completely before frosting.

9. To make the frosting, beat the butter with an electric mixer until it is smooth. Add the salt and vanilla and beat until well mixed.

10. Add the powdered sugar and 2 tbsp of milk. Beat until well blended, starting slowly and gradually increasing the speed of the mixer to high.

11. Add more milk or powdered sugar to improve the consistency if needed.

12. Beat in the cinnamon.

13. Frost the cake and decorate as desired.

This moist cake will keep at room temperature for several days.

Grapefruit Chiffon Cake

Prep Time: 30 mins

Cook Time: 45 mins

Total Time: 1 hour 15 mins

Yield: 12 servings

Nutritional Information per Serving:

Total Calories	Carbohydrates	Fat	Protein
278	35.1 g	12.6 g	6.7 g

Ingredients:

- 1 2/3 cup all-purpose flour
- 1 cup granulated sugar, divided in half
- 2 tsp baking powder
- zest of 1 medium grapefruit
- 8 large eggs
- 1/2 cup vegetable oil
- 1/3 cup whole milk
- 1/3 cup grapefruit juice
- 2 tsp vanilla extract
- 1 tsp mezcal (optional)

Topping:

- 1 cup granulated sugar, divided in half
- 1/2 cup water
- 6 oz (170 g) fresh cranberries
- fresh rosemary

Glaze:

- 4–5 tbsp grapefruit juice
- 2 cups powdered sugar

Directions:

1. Preheat the oven to 350 °F (180 °C).
2. Separate the eggs, placing the whites in a bowl (or the bowl of a stand mixer), and the yolks in another large bowl. Ensure that there is no yolk mixed in with the whites.
3. Add 1/2 cup of the sugar, together with the milk, grapefruit juice, mezcal, and vegetable oil to the egg

yolks. Whisk until well combined. Sift in the flour and baking powder and mix until combined. Make sure there are no lumps. After whisking in the vanilla extract, set aside.

4. Beat the egg whites with an electric beater or stand mixer until foamy. Increase the speed of the beater or mixer and gradually add the remaining sugar. Whisk the egg whites into stiff peaks. Make sure you don't overbeat.

5. Add a third of the egg whites to the yolk mixture. Fold them in gently with a spatula until well combined. Add the rest of the whites and fold them in until well combined. You should see no egg white streaks. Do not overmix to maintain the air in the egg whites.

6. Carefully pour the batter into a 10 in. (20 cm) angel food tube cake pan with a removable bottom (don't use non-stick ones). Run a long skewer through the batter a few times. Very gently, tap the bottom of the pan on a hard surface to remove any air bubbles.

7. Bake for 45 minutes. If the cake is fully baked, a skewer or small knife should come out clean.

8. Remove from the oven and carefully turn the cake in the pan upside down so the middle tube is balanced on an overturned bowl. Let it cool completely.

9. Carefully remove the cake from the pan. You can run a small knife along the edges to loosen it. Place the cake right-side up on a plate.

Making the Topping:

1. In a small saucepan, heat the sugar and water until the sugar dissolves completely. Leave it to cool entirely. Mix the cranberries into this syrup and spoon them onto a baking rack.

2. After about 45 minutes, roll them in the powdered sugar to coat. Wait an hour for them to set before using.
3. To make the glaze, combine the grapefruit juice and powdered sugar until it is thick and smooth but pours easily.
4. Pour it evenly over the cake and top it with the sugared cranberries. Garnish with rosemary sprigs.

Grilled Pineapple With Cream

Prep Time: 20 mins

Cook Time: 25 mins

Total Time: 45 mins

Yield: 4 servings

Nutritional Information per Serving:

Total Calories	Carbohydrates	Fat	Protein
254	26 g	16 g	1 g

Ingredients:

- 1 large pineapple
- 1 tbsp dark agave syrup
- 2 limes
- 2 tbsp mezcal
- 1 tbsp olive oil
- pinch kosher salt
- whipped cream
- reserved lime zest
- 1 cup heavy cream
- 1 tbsp dark agave syrup (plus extra for serving)

- 10 mint leaves (optional, for serving)

Directions:

1. Peel and core the pineapple. Slice it into 1 in. (2 cm) rounds and place them in a large bowl.
2. Grate the lime skins and reserve the zest to add to the whipped cream later. Juice the limes.
3. Combine the lime juice, mezcal, agave syrup, and salt in a small bowl. Pour over the pineapple and toss gently until the fruit is coated. Leave to stand for 20 minutes.
4. Preheat the grill or a grill pan over medium heat.
5. Brush the grill with the olive oil and grill the pineapple slices for about 3 minutes per side. Ensure that the pineapple stays firm. Set aside after grilling.
6. Fit a whisk attachment to an electric mixer. Place the cream, lime zest, and agave syrup in a bowl. Whisk for about 2–3 minutes, until stiff peaks form.
7. For serving, top the grilled pineapple with the whipped cream. Drizzle with more agave syrup. Garnish with mint leaves if desired.

MEZCAL DRINKS AND COCKTAILS

Oaxacan Coffee

Prep Time: 6 mins

Mixing Time: 3 mins

Total Time: 9 mins

Yield: 1 serving

Nutritional Information per Serving:

Total Calories

Total Calories	Carbohydrates	Fat	Protein
228	10 g	9.3 g	0.8 g

Ingredients:

- 3–4 oz (90–120 ml) freshly brewed black filter coffee
- 1 1/2 oz (45 ml) mezcal
- 1 tsp brown sugar or brown sugar simple syrup
- ice
- dash chocolate mole bitters or chopped Mexican chocolate (optional)

Topping:

- whipped cream

Directions:

1. Brew fresh, black, medium-roast coffee. Set aside 3–4 oz (90–120 ml). If you are using brown sugar, add it to the coffee and stir it in well.
2. When the coffee has cooled, pour it into a shaker.
3. Add the rest of the ingredients to the shaker (omit the syrup if you have already added sugar to the coffee).
4. Shake well until all the ingredients are well mixed.
5. Pour into a glass, straining it as you go to catch the ice.
6. Add more coffee or syrup to taste.
7. Top with a dollop of whipped cream.

Spicy Hot Chocolate With Chili, Cinnamon, and Mezcal

Prep Time: 5 mins

Cook Time: 10 mins

Total Time: 15 mins

Yield: 4 servings

Nutritional Information per Serving:

Total Calories	Carbohydrates	Fat	Protein
566	31 g	35 g	14 g

Ingredients:

- 1/4 cup cocoa powder
- 2 cups whole milk
- 5 oz (120 ml) mezcal
- 1 tbsp granulated sugar
- pinch kosher salt
- 6 cinnamon sticks
- 1 whole ancho chili pod, dried and split
- 8 oz (227 g) bittersweet chocolate chips
- garnish options: Chile powder, cocoa nib, dark chocolate shavings

Directions:

1. In a saucepan, mix the cocoa powder, sugar, and salt. Add the milk, cinnamon sticks, chili, and bittersweet chocolate. Heat over medium heat, stirring continuously, until the chocolate melts.

2. Whisk gently to ensure that everything is well blended. Simmer over low heat until the mixture is fragrant, about 10 minutes. Be careful not to let it boil over.

3. Remove the mixture from the heat and pour it into a heatproof jug (through a strainer to remove the solids). Discard the solids. Pour the milk mixture back into the pot.

4. Add the mezcal and heat through.

5. Beat the drink until foamy using a hand blender or whisk.

6. Pour into mugs and garnish with one of the above options. Add a cinnamon stick to each mug if you wish.

7. Serve immediately.

Oaxaca Old Fashioned Cocktail

Mixing Time: 2 mins

Total Time: 2 mins

Yield: 1 serving

Nutritional Information per Serving:

Total Calories	Carbohydrates	Fat	Protein
154	6 g	0 g	0 g

Ingredients:

- 1 1/2 oz (45 ml) reposado tequila
- 1/2 oz (15 ml) mezcal joven
- 1–2 dashes Angostura bitters
- 1 tsp agave nectar
- long twist orange peel for garnish

Directions:

1. Add all ingredients to a glass container for mixing, and top off with ice.
2. Stir until chilled and strain into an old fashioned glass.
3. Twist the orange peel over the drink as a garnish.
4. For a dramatic effect, you can light the orange peel so the oils alight.

Smoky Oaxacan Mezcal and Basil Cocktail

Mixing Time: 10 mins

Total Time: 10 mins

Yield: 1 serving

Nutritional Information per Serving:

Total Calories	Carbohydrates	Fat	Protein
290	42 g	1 g	1 g

Ingredients:

- 2 oz (60 ml) mezcal
- 1 1/2 oz (45 ml) lime juice
- 5 basil leaves
- 3 lime wedges
- 1 1/2 oz (45 ml) agave syrup
- ice
- bacon salt (for the glass rim)
- extra basil leaves and lime wedge for garnish

Directions:

1. In a shaker, muddle the lime wedges and basil leaves.
2. Add the lime juice, mezcal, agave syrup, and ice. Shake well.
3. Run a lime wedge around the rim of the glass and roll the rim in the bacon salt.
4. Add ice to the glass and pour in the cocktail.
5. Garnish with basil leaves and a lime wedge.
6. Serve immediately.

Peach Mezcal Margarita

Mixing Time: 5 mins

Total Time: 5 mins

Yield: 1 serving

Nutritional Information per Serving:

Total Calories	Carbohydrates	Fat	Protein
207	13 g	1 g	1 g

Ingredients:

- 1/2 peach
- 2 oz (60 ml) mezcal
- 1/2 oz (15 ml) lime juice
- 1/2 oz (15 ml) triple sec
- ice

Directions:

1. Peel the peach and chop it up. Put it into a blender. Add the mezcal, lime juice, and triple sec.
2. Pulse until well blended.
3. Add ice to a serving glass and pour the cocktail over it.
4. Stir to cool.
5. Serve with a peach slice to garnish.

Basil Julep With Cucumber, Jalapeño, and Mezcal (El Derby Ahumado)

Mixing Time: 5 mins

Total Time: 5 mins

Yield: 1 serving

Nutritional Information per Serving:

Total Calories	Carbohydrates	Fat	Protein
200	18 g	0 g	0 g

Ingredients:

- 1 1/2 oz (45 ml) mezcal
- 2 tsp agave syrup
- 1 slice (1/2 in. or 1 cm thick) cucumber
- 1 thin slice jalapeño pepper (the thickness will determine how spicy the flavor is)
- 6 fresh basil leaves, plus a tuft of basil sprigs
- crushed or shaved ice
- cucumber stick for garnish

Directions:

1. Muddle the cucumber and jalapeño slices in a julep cup or rocks glass until they are thoroughly crushed and have released all their juices.
2. Add the basil leaves and agave syrup and continue muddling until the basil is lightly bruised.
3. Take the basil leaves and wipe the inside of the glass with them to impart their aromatic oils to the drink.
4. Add the mezcal. Half-fill the glass with crushed ice and stir to combine.
5. Top off the glass with crushed ice and stir until the outside of the glass becomes frosty.
6. Add more crushed ice, heaping it a little.
7. Garnish with the cucumber stick and basil sprigs.
8. Serve with a short straw so the basil bouquet will be released as the drinker sips.

Mezcal Mule

Mixing Time: 5 mins

Total Time: 5 mins

Yield: 1 serving

Nutritional Information per Serving:

Total Calories	Carbohydrates	Fat	Protein
200	18 g	0 g	0 g

Ingredients:

- 1 1/2 oz (45 ml) mezcal
- 3/4 oz (20 ml) lime juice, freshly squeezed
- 3/4 oz (20 ml) passion fruit purée
- 3 cucumber slices
- ginger beer, chilled
- additional cucumber slice, candied ginger, chili powder (for garnish)

Directions:

1. Muddle the cucumber slices and agave nectar in a shaker.
2. Add the lime juice, mezcal, and passion fruit purée. Top up with ice.
3. Shake until the mixture is well chilled.
4. Add fresh ice to a rocks glass and strain the mixture over it.
5. Top up with ginger beer.
6. Garnish with a cucumber slice and a piece of candied ginger. Add a pinch of chili powder to the top.

After trying your hand at some mezcal-infused Mexican dishes, you may decide to concoct your own versions of favorite recipes. Slow-cooking, and what I call Togetherness-Cooking© (see my upcoming book on the topic) are becoming increasingly popular in a world that has been seared by Covid-isolation, disposable culture, and take-out diets. Lighthearted banter, meaningful conversation, and even companionable silence help build relationships when you tackle a good project with others. The kitchen is the perfect place for feelings of kinship and community to develop. While the food is cooking, and before you taste together mezcal's unique contribution to your *chef d'oeuvre*, you may bring up the topic of mezcal pairings and share ideas about how to make your next dinner or gathering even more memorable. Sooner or later, the conversation is sure to turn to health concerns. Mezcal, after all, is an alcoholic beverage and may not be right for everyone (unless it has been cooked in one of your dishes, of course)! What few realize, however, is that mezcal does have some surprising health benefits. In the next chapter, we will delve into this bold assertion.

HEALTHY SIPPING

> *El amor tocó a mi puerta, pero yo ya había salido por un mezcal.*
>
> Love knocked on my door, but I had already gone out for a mezcal.
>
> — MEXICAN EXPRESSION

> *Take the tiniest sip you can possibly take and squeeze your tongue into the roof of your mouth and into the front of your teeth and the mezcal will go to the back of your tongue and over your palate and down the throat. Wait 30 seconds before taking another sip, and your palate will be awakened. After that, sip normally and the mezcal will be softer and sweeter. Once you've consumed mezcal three or four times, you won't have to tune up your palate because you'll know what you're expecting. The motto is: Sip it. Don't shoot it.*
>
> — RON COOPER

Did you know that you can drink mezcal as part of a health-conscious diet, including Paleo? The good news is that, rather like red wine and when consumed in modest quantities, mezcal has definite health benefits. You'll find out more about those in this chapter.

AGAVE SPIRITS IN THE PALEO DIET

The diet was named after the *Paleolithic* people, whom we envision toiling as hunter-gatherers, surviving on meat, fish, and foraged eggs, fruit, nuts, or seeds. Proponents of the diet exclude processed or refined foods and drinks that obviously weren't available to a Stone-Age population. Assuming a nomadic lifestyle for the early people, they also eschew nutrition sourced from cultivated crops or domesticated animals.

Adherents of the Paleo diet contend that food produced with supplemental processing or animal husbandry is not processed effectively by the human body and may contribute to conditions like diabetes, heart disease, and obesity. Of course, the hard work required to eke out a bare-bone existence with primitive tools and defend one's meager cache from wild animals and aggressive rival bands, as well as the never-ending moves to new areas in search of safety, acceptable weather, or available food can scarce be compared to our sedentary lifestyles and their resultant ailments.

Foods in the Paleo Diet

As mentioned previously, the Paleo diet includes (Mayo Clinic Staff, 2020):

- protein derived from lean meats, such as grass-fed livestock or wild game, together with omega-3-rich fish, such as albacore tuna, mackerel, and salmon, as well as eggs.

- fruits, vegetables, nuts, and seeds that provide vitamins, minerals, and fiber
- oil derived directly from fruits and nuts, such as olive oil or avocado oil
- herbs and spices that add flavor to food
- water, with coffee and tea in moderation

Foods to be avoided on the Paleo diet include:

- legumes (e.g., beans, peas, lentils, peanuts), grains (e.g., wheat, oats, barley, and their derivatives, such as bread, pasta, and spelt)
- most dairy products, especially low-fat options (e.g., milk, cheese, yogurt)
- refined or added sugar and salt
- starchy vegetables, such as corn, peas, and white potatoes
- agriculturally produced vegetable oils, including soybean, sunflower, cottonseed, corn, grapeseed, and safflower
- processed foods, such as chips, cookies, soft drinks, and artificial sweeteners

In general, industrially produced foods should be eaten sparingly.

Rather than being an absolutist creed that must be followed to the letter, the Paleo diet can serve as a helpful framework for evaluating the major food groups in one's diet. For example, you might select grass-fed butter or gluten-free grains, or you might dramatically increase the proportion of lean meat and fish in your diet for a fixed period of time.

Individuals who have digestive issues should consult their doctors or health practitioners before embarking on the Paleo diet, as it is high in fiber. Vegetarians and vegans might have additional challenges because legumes form an important part of their diets.

Red Wine and the Paleo Diet

Indulgences like dark chocolate and red wine are beneficial and can be enjoyed, albeit sparingly, by followers of the Paleo diet. Beer, on the other hand, is not generally recommended, as it has usually been brewed from cultivated grains. Alternatives such as gluten-free and grain-free beers are becoming available, and some Paleo diet adherents consume them.

Red wine contains antioxidants and anti-inflammatory compounds, including resveratrol, which are highly beneficial to human health. This is one of the reasons it has been included in the Paleo diet. Several other beneficial polyphenols, antioxidants found in wine, occur there naturally and in plenty. Polyphenols reduce oxidative stress in the body. They ensure a healthy gut biome because they are high in beneficial bacterial strains, and they neutralize dangerous free radicals, which are known to damage living tissues. There is also copious evidence that polyphenols also protect the heart from damage, prevent certain cancers, and raise levels of beneficial HDL cholesterol while they control harmful LDL cholesterol (Cory et al, 2018). Polyphenols help regulate metabolism, control weight, and may have preventive and therapeutic effects on some chronic diseases. Keep in mind that these attributes are a net benefit to health when red wine is consumed in moderation, but are more than offset by oxidative stress if you drink to excess.

Red wine contains more beneficial elements than white wine, possibly in part because the grapes used to make red wine are left to hang longer on the vine. The primary reason, however, is that grape skins are included during the fermentation process. To make white wine, however, the grapes are crushed and their skins removed before fermentation. Anthocyanins, which give red wine its deep color, are a group of antioxidants that can help protect our brains and defend our bodies against many chronic diseases. Phenolic compounds in red wine have been demonstrated to exhibit beneficial effects on human health, due to their anti-inflammatory and antioxidant properties and their role in tissue repair processes (Markoski et al, 2016).

Wine Choices for Paleo

To complement the food on a Paleo diet, select wines that have fewer natural sugars. Reduced or no-alcohol wines can also be consumed.

Wine options for Paleo aficionados include full-bodied reds, such as Cabernet, Malbec, Merlot, Pinot Noir, Sangiovese, and Zinfandel. Although white wines are not recommended, the occasional glass won't be an issue. Focus on drier Sauvignon Blanc or Pinot Grigio, while avoiding very sweet Rieslings or Moscatos.

Even if you are on the Paleo diet, you can still pair your food with fine wines by using the guidelines below (Alcohol Free Wellness, 2022):

- Pinot Noir is versatile and can be consumed with just about any food, although it is particularly enjoyable with roast chicken.
- Cabernet is a bold red wine that complements lean red meats or wild game. Enjoy it with grilled steaks or kebabs.
- Sparkling rosé wines are a good choice for Paleo. Pair them with fish or salads. Low-alcohol and no-alcohol options are available.
- Sauvignon Blanc is a low-sugar white wine that

complements foods such as chicken, shellfish, stir-fries, and dishes based on rice and noodles.

Wine has much less alcohol by volume than mezcal, and it has abundant acidity, *tannins*, and fruit notes. Mezcal has much lower acidity, lower tannins, and lacks the fruity structure of fermented grapes. You can pick either wine or mezcal when selecting an *apéritif* or a *digestif*, but be sure to cleanse your palate between sips as each each type of beverage has its own oral chemistry, and they are not compatible with each other. For the same reason, you should pause and sip water between a savory dinner *entrée* and a sweet dessert. Still or sparkling water is the easiest way to cleanse, but you can also reset your mouth to neutral with a bite of mild bread, unsalted crackers, or fruit served at room temperature.

Mezcal and the Paleo Diet

I have wonderful news for you. Agave spirits are compatible with the Paleo diet! Mezcal, tequila, and pulque all come from agave and cleanly fit the framework for Paleo. Mezcal is a great option for those who value traditional production processes that do not entail the synthetic ingredients so frequently found in other beverages.

Today, mezcal is still primarily fermented in vats made of wood, clay, and other natural materials that can confer additional benefits. Mezcal is also gluten-free and high in antioxidants.

HEALTH BENEFITS OF MEZCAL

If you're watching your weight, you'll be pleased to learn that neat mezcal has the lowest calorie count of any alcohol. The worms at the bottom of your glasses or in some bottles of mezcal are edible. Besides contributing to the unique flavor profiles of such mezcals, the worms are a concentrated protein source. *Maguey worms*, as they're known in Mexico, are often roasted or deep-fried and added to tortilla fillings.

Because mezcal is made from agaves, it contains many of the bioactive compounds found in these succulents. These compounds are beneficial to your body. Agave plants contain a probiotic called *agavin*, which is usually present in the mash added to fermentation vats. Besides aiding in fermentation, agavin is also found in the final product. This means that drinking mezcal in moderation could benefit your gut microbiome.

Mezcal contains aromatic compounds or *terpenes* derived from agave plants. Several studies, mainly conducted on mice and other rodents, suggest that these compounds might be beneficial to humans who consume agave-derived beverages such as mezcal. However, I am not aware of any human studies that have confirmed these effects. Below are a few highlights from the studies (Taylor, 2020):

- Research conducted in 2015 found that geraniol has antidepressant properties and is effective in reducing stress in mice. We do not know if humans also experience these benefits from drinking mezcal or from consuming other foods and drinks that contain geraniol, although a little mezcal and a little music might lift your mood. Mezcal could also help you sleep, although it's best not to consume alcoholic beverages too close to bedtime to ensure an uninterrupted night's sleep.

- Mezcal is the only agave-based alcoholic beverage to contain limonene. In 2018, laboratory studies indicated that this compound might have anti-cancer effects but their efficacy in the real world is unknown. Alternative health practitioners also use limonene to treat bronchitis or obesity, but I am not aware of any scientific findings supporting its use for these purposes.

- Citronellol, which occurs in agave and other plants, was found in 2020 to relax blood vessels in rats. This lowered their blood pressure. Whether mezcal drinkers experience the same effects remains to be seen.

- Most of us have heard about free radicals. These are unstable atoms created when oxygen molecules disintegrate inside the body. They steal electrons from the body's cells when this happens, leading to oxidative stress. This has been linked to several chronic diseases and conditions. Scientists have found that eugenol, another terpene found in agave, maintains the integrity of oxygen molecules, binding to free radicals and preventing oxidative stress in humans.

- A 2018 scientific paper records that farnesol, another terpene found in agaves, might have anti-inflammatory properties. However, consuming excessive amounts of alcohol can promote inflammation in the body, so moderate consumption of mezcal is key to deriving these benefits.
- Agaves, and by extension mezcal, contain fructans, a type of carbohydrate found in plants. A 2014 study found that fructans in agave may prevent bone loss by raising calcium concentrations in both the blood and bones, encouraging the formation of new bone. The study was conducted on mice, but consuming mezcal might also confer these benefits on humans.

DISADVANTAGES OF DRINKING MEZCAL

While drinking mezcal regularly can be beneficial overall, there are some ways in which it can negatively impact your health. Most of these can be avoided by ensuring that you always consume mezcal in extreme moderation.

Although mezcal is one of the purest alcoholic spirits, like other alcoholic beverages, it contains traces of ethyl carbamate, which is released during fermentation. Laboratory studies have found that ethyl carbamate is a carcinogen that may cause lung, liver, and blood cancers. Whether mezcal's concentration of healthful limonene is sufficient to overcome the traces of ethyl carbamate is unknown. Individuals at risk for developing cancer should probably avoid alcoholic drinks in any event. The good news is that a

2009 scientific analysis of agave-based spirits, including tequila and mezcal, found that their ethyl carbamate concentrations were within international safety guidelines (Taylor, 2020).

We live in a world in which there are no perfectly clean or healthy foods or beverages. Even organically-grown apples can contain substantial amounts of naturally-occurring carcinogens such as *patulin*. The important thing is to strive for balance, recognizing that hints of natural toxins are more than overcome by healthy antioxidants, vitamins, and anodyne compounds which impel your body towards greater wellness. It is possible that the phenomenon of *hormesis* mitigates exposure to minor chemical insults without diluting the benefit of protective compounds which are abundant in nutritious sustenance.

Another potential threat to the health of those who drink too much mezcal is the development of kidney stones. Agave-based spirits all contain relatively high quantities of *oxalates*, which are also found in many other edible plants. Oxalates bind calcium and other minerals together, which can create kidney stones. If you are concerned about kidney stones or have suffered from them before, you might want to limit your mezcal consumption.

Strict vegetarians or vegans might not be able to consume all mezcals. Besides avoiding brands that might contain worms, they might need to avoid drinking *pechuga* mezcal, as it is made by hanging a raw chicken breast inside the distillation still. While the chicken breast cooks, it releases juices and fats that give the mezcal a robust flavor and savory notes.

TIPS FOR CONSUMING MEZCAL AS PART OF A HEALTHY LIFESTYLE

As with many other pleasurable and even beneficial experiences in life, you can have too much of a good thing. Drinking mezcal is no exception. Healthy drinking means moderating your consumption, so you can enjoy the benefits without suffering the negatives. There is an easy rule of thumb to stay on the safe side of alcohol consumption: No more than one drink per day for women and no more than two drinks a day for men is the typical recommendation. In addition to all the pitfalls of excessive consumption, alcoholic drinks have a diuretic effect, so make sure that you drink plenty of water to remain adequately hydrated. Additionally, they should not be consumed within three hours of sleep, as this could disrupt your sleep patterns (Bryan and Singh, 2024).

Guidelines for drinking mezcal as part of a healthy lifestyle include (Didonato, 2022):

- limiting syrups, sweet mixers, and sugary sodas or sweetened tonic water
- consuming cocktails with less than two ingredients, i.e., mezcal plus one other beverage
- drinking high-quality mezcal
- adding hydrating mixers such as water or soda water
- focusing on herbal and vegetable garnishes such as basil, cucumber, lemon, lime, ginger, mint, or rosemary (to impart additional flavors)

MEZCAL-BASED COCKTAILS FOR PALEO

In this section, you'll find a range of low-carb, low-sugar recipes based on natural ingredients that are perfect for the Paleo diet.

Keto Margarita

Prep Time: 1 min

Mixing Time: 1 min

Total Time: 2 mins

Yield: 2 servings

Nutritional Information per Serving:

Total Calories	Carbohydrates	Fat	Protein
104	2 g	1 g	1 g

Ingredients:

- 3 tbsp lime juice
- 3 oz (90 ml) mezcal
- 1/2 cup seltzer, water, or soda water
- 1/4 cup ice
- 1/2 tsp orange extract
- 1 tbsp keto simple syrup or keto maple syrup
- 1/4 cup fresh or frozen strawberries (optional)
- Sliced limes for garnish

Directions:

1. Pour all the ingredients into a cocktail shaker.
2. Shake vigorously for 1–2 minutes.

3. Pour into 2 glasses.
4. Serve with freshly sliced limes.

Mezcal Ranch Water

Prep Time: 3 mins

Mixing Time: 2 mins

Total Time: 5 mins

Yield: 2 servings

Nutritional Information per Serving:

Total Calories	Carbohydrates	Fat	Protein
207	4 g	1 g	1 g

Ingredients:

- 6 oz (180 ml) mezcal
- 2 bottles sparkling mineral water (such as Topo Chico, Sanpellegrino, or Perrier)
- juice of 2 limes, about 3 oz (90 ml)
- *tajín*
- ice

Directions:

1. Run a lime wedge down one side of each glass on the inside.
2. Pour tajín on this part of the glass; it should stick to the lime juice.
3. Add ice to each glass until they are about 3/4 full.

4. Divide the mezcal and lime juice evenly between the glasses.
5. Top up with sparkling mineral water.
6. Garnish with a lime slice.

Prosecco Margaritas

This recipe makes several margaritas and can be mixed in advance.

Prep Time: 15 mins

Mixing Time: 5 mins

Total Time: 20 mins

Yield: 4–6 margaritas

Nutritional Information per Serving:

Total Calories	Carbohydrates	Fat	Protein
156	101 g	0 g	1 g

Ingredients:

- 3 oz (90 ml) blanco tequila
- 8 oz (240 ml) lime juice, freshly squeezed
- 3 oz (90 ml) Cointreau
- 25 oz (750 ml) bottle Prosecco (dry or demi-sec)
- 4 oz (120 ml) agave syrup (or to taste)
- garnish options: coarse salt, fresh lime wedges or slices

Directions:

1. Mix the tequila, fresh lime juice, Cointreau, and agave syrup together in a lidded jar or pitcher. Let it stand until you are ready to serve.
2. To salt the glass rims, run a lime juice wedge over them and dip the rims in a small plate of coarse salt.
3. Cut the limes into wedges or slices and place them on a covered plate in the fridge.
4. To serve, add ice to the glasses. Stir the margarita mix to combine and divide evenly into the glasses. Add the Prosecco last.
5. Stir lightly and taste. Add more syrup or lime as needed.
6. Garnish with lime wedges or slices.

Jalapeño Mezcal Margarita

Prep Time: 20 mins

Total Time: 20 mins

Yield: 1 margarita

Nutritional Information per Serving:

Total Calories	Carbohydrates	Fat	Protein
1,087	42 g	2 g	4 g

Ingredients:

Jalapeño mezcal:

- 2 cups mezcal
- 6 slices jalapeño, 1/4 in. (1/4 cm) thick

Rim salt:

- 1 tbsp chili powder
- 2 tbsp kosher salt
- 1/4 tsp ground black pepper
- 1/8 tsp chipotle powder
- fresh lime wedge
- coarsely ground black pepper

Margarita:

- 2 oz (60 ml) lime juice, freshly squeezed
- 2 oz (60 ml) prepared jalapeño mezcal
- 3–4 drops orange bitters
- 1/2 oz (15 ml) Cointreau
- 1/2 tsp honey
- chopped ice
- garnish: lime wedge and jalapeño slice

Directions:

1. Pour the mezcal into a pint jar and add the jalapeño slices.
2. Cover and refrigerate overnight.
3. Remove the jalapeño slices in the morning or leave them in longer for a spicier mezcal.
4. To rim the glasses, combine the salt ingredients in a small bowl.
5. Transfer to a small plate.
6. Run the cut side of a lemon wedge around the rim of a 10 oz (250 ml) glass.
7. Dip the damp rim into the chili salt and set the glass aside.
8. To create the margarita, pour some jalapeño mezcal into the prepared glass. Add the lime juice, Cointreau, orange

bitters, and honey. Stir thoroughly until the honey is totally incorporated.

9. Fill the glass with chopped ice and stir to combine.
10. Garnish with a lime wedge and jalapeño slice.

Mezcal Margarita

Prep Time: 5 mins

Total Time: 5 mins

Yield: 2 servings

Nutritional Information per Serving:

Total Calories	Carbohydrates	Fat	Protein
200	4 g	1 g	1 g

Ingredients:

- 3 oz (90 ml) lime juice, freshly squeezed (5–6 limes)
- 3 oz (90 ml) mezcal or tequila
- 2 tbsp honey or agave nectar
- 4 tbsp water
- ice cubes
- 1/8 tsp salt or to taste
- lime slices for garnish

Directions:

1. In a small saucepan, heat the honey or agave nectar and water over high heat. After 5 mins, the mixture should have reached a syrupy consistency. Remove from the heat and allow to cool.

2. Mix the honey syrup, together with the mezcal and fresh lime juice, in a cocktail shaker.
3. Shake well.
4. Add ice cubes to a glass and pour the cocktail over them. Alternatively, serve neat.
5. Garnish with a lime slice.

SELECTING HIGH-QUALITY MEZCAL FOR HEALTH

Drinking mezcal for health reasons means consuming superior-quality spirits. But how do you know that you're drinking the best? What should you look for? Below are a few pointers (La Luna Mezcal, 2022; Newman, 2023):

- Read the label. Most mezcal bottles have detailed labels that reveal a great deal about the contents. The more information appears on a label, the easier making an informed choice will be. Additionally, a thorough description makes it more likely that the mezcal will be of good quality. The labels on mezcal from certified producers should include the following: the agave species used and when applicable, their percentages in the bottle as well as details about additional compounds, the type and category of mezcal, the alcohol content, and the name of the production region.
- Visit brands' websites to find out more about their products.
- The best Mexican mezcals are produced in states that fall within the DO. Not only do they have the exclusive right to use the name *mezcal*, but producers are also subject to stringent certification requirements that verify production methods.

- The species of agave used also affects the quality of the mezcal. Look for the following:

  - Maguey Americano
  - Maguey Azul
  - Maguey Cenizo
  - Maguey Espadin
  - Maguey Jabalí
  - Maguey Largo
  - Maguey Lechuguilla
  - Maguey Papalote o Cupreata

- The spirit should be thick and dense. You can usually see this by looking at the bottle but you can also shake it a little to check. If the mezcal stays on the walls of the bottle and runs down slowly, then it is likely of superior quality.
- When you shake the bottle a little harder, pearl-shaped bubbles should appear on top of the liquid. This is another sign of a good mezcal.
- The spirit should have a high alcohol concentration. On labels, this is referred to as ethanol or ethyl alcohol. In mezcal, these are usually between 35% and 55% according to industry standards, which is high for an alcoholic beverage.
- A good mezcal should smell smoky because of the process used to make it. If it doesn't have that aroma, it's probably not of high quality—or it's not artisanal mezcal. Put a drop on the back of your hand and inhale it slowly. You should be able to smell the characteristic aromas of a good mezcal.

We have seen that mezcal is a unique spirit containing many compounds that may be beneficial to human health. When consumed with care and in moderation, mezcal can potentially deliver these health benefits and can even form part of the Paleo diet.

In the next chapter, you'll learn how to grow your own agaves in your own backyard, to use in the production of your own mezcal.

CULTIVATING AGAVE AT HOME

> *The desert works constantly to forbid it, and still the cactus blooms.*

— UMA GOKHALE

> *A forest is a mystery, but the desert is truth.*

— KEITH MILLER

In this chapter, you'll find out how to go about sourcing agaves, as well as how to cultivate them in your garden or on your smallholding or farm. By the end of this chapter, you should be able to confidently grow and harvest agave plants for home mezcal-making.

Although you will be growing them primarily for mezcal-making, it's worth remembering that agaves make great landscaping plants, with a striking range of leaf shapes, sizes, and colors. Like most succulents, agaves have fleshy leaves with colors varying from blue-gray to green, and you can even get variegated varieties. As mentioned previously, these are extremely long-lived plants. If you grow your own, you'll need to wait for several years before you can cut off the leaves and harvest the inner core to make mezcal. In the meantime, you will be able to enjoy the exotic beauty of the agave.

AGAVE BASICS: PLANT DESCRIPTION

Agave plants are not difficult to identify, as they have very distinctive shapes and forms. Here are a few pointers as to what to look for (Vorderbruggen, 2008):

Leaves

Agave leaves form a rosette around the plant with the leaves emanating from the plant's base. Leaves are usually long and narrow, tapering to a pointed, hardened tip. Leaf veins run parallel to one another. Like most succulents, agaves bear thick, fleshy leaves that are usually two to five feet in length. The leaves are smooth and usually have toothed edges, often equipped with sharp spines. Within their blue-green spectrum, these leaves are a multi-dimensional panorama that brings a vivid landscape to your home. Multihued or variegated agave can be especially spectacular. Agaves grow around one hundred and thirty leaves in seven years. They drop to the ground when they die, helping to retain soil moisture (*Agave Growth and Harvesting,* 2022).

Agave americana, the variety most often used for mezcal production in the United States, has gray-green leaves that measure up to two feet in length. The mature plant is about four feet wide. It lives for approximately ten to thirty years (Francis, 2015).

Stems

The stem is what you will use to produce your mezcal. It is round and thick, usually forming the base of the rosette, and reaches a height of 11–19 inches (30–50 centimeters). After six years of growth, the stem weighs around 66 pounds (30 kilograms). When the plant starts flowering, the stem lengthens (*Agave Growth and Harvesting*, 2022).

Flowers

When mature, the agave sends up an incredibly long flower stem. Depending on the species, this stem can be as high as thirty feet tall (*Agave Growth and Harvesting*, 2022). At the top of the flower stalk is a cluster of small flowers on short branches. The flowers are usually yellow or white, depending on the species.

Fruit and Seeds

Agave fruits are usually capsules or berries that contain oval black or brown seeds. They are surprisingly small.

A NOTE ABOUT WILD AGAVE FORAGING

Before you grab your hiking boots and pruning shears, it's important to cover some ground rules about foraging for agave in the wild.

In some places, such as California, harvesting wild agave is illegal on public lands. Of course, you should first obtain a landowner's permission before harvesting naturally-growing agave on private land. It's important to familiarize yourself with local regulations if you intend to harvest wild agaves, so you do not run afoul of the law.

If you wish to harvest on someone else's private land, consider offering to facilitate the planting of more agave in exchange for what you harvest, and if you own enough suitable land, consider planting your own!

Agave is a low-maintenance crop and the end result is well worth the wait. If you fertilize your plants once a season, they will also develop faster, which means that you could reduce your time from planting to harvest from eight years on average to five to six years (English, 2012).

Wild agaves that reproduce naturally from seed pollinated by birds and bats are more genetically diverse than agaves derived from pups or bulbils, which means that they are better able to withstand adverse environmental conditions and are more resistant to pests or diseases than their cloned cousins. Because they are such long-lived plants, agaves are often an essential component of the ecosystems in which they are found, providing food, shelter, and other resources for regional birds and wildlife. Please practice good stewardship, and make sure you leave plenty of agave to replenish the landscape in future years.

CULTIVATING AGAVES IN YOUR OWN SPACE

Cultivating agave is an excellent option if you have enough space. Keep in mind that many of the varieties that are suitable for making mezcal grow to very large sizes.

Precautions

When working with your plants, be careful not to get the raw sap on your skin, as it is an irritant and can burn the skin, eyes, and other exposed parts of your body. These burns take a long time to heal, so it's better to avoid getting them in the first place. This is agave, not aloe vera!

Agaves are very spiky, so wear thick gloves when handling young plants and be careful around them so you aren't scraped. Some plants also have spines down the center of the leaves. Wash your hands and forearms after handling agaves to remove any traces of sap that might have been deposited on your skin.

The spot that you select to locate your agaves must be large enough to accommodate the future mature plants. Make sure that, when fully grown, those plants won't interfere with structures, trees, or larger plants. Agaves have enormous *taproots*, and transplanting them is not an option, so it's essential to plant them in the right place from the start.

Keep in mind that herbivorous animals may find your agaves attractive, just as deer may find your vegetable garden desirable. It's a good idea to fence off your planting from local wildlife and domestic stock.

Soil Requirements

Agaves flourish best when planted in deep soils with a neutral pH (the measure of acidity and alkalinity) between six and seven (Cortes, 2021). Loamy soils are best. If your soil tends to be sandy or clay, you might need to add compost and lime on occasion. By far the most important requirement for growing agave is that your property should not be prone to flooding or water logging during the rainy season. Agaves naturally thrive in more arid climates and soils, so excessive moisture will adversely affect their root development.

Best Agave Varieties to Grow for Mezcal

When choosing an agave variety for your homemade mezcal, consider your local climate, soils, temperatures, rainfall patterns, and how much space you have, as certain varieties grow into enormous plants. Growing agaves for mezcal-making is a long-term project, so plan accordingly.

Below is a list of suggested agave species and varieties you could cultivate in your garden (McEvoy, 2013):

Botanical Name	Suggested Varieties
Agave americana L. var. oaxacensis	Arroqueño Blanco Maguey de Coyote Sierra Negra
Agave americana	Americana Mezcal Serrano
Agave angustifolia	Espadin
Agave asperrima Jacobi	Bruto o Cenizo Maguey de Cerro
Agave ciereago	Ciereago
Agave cupreata	Maguey Papalote
Agave de Lumbre	de Lumbre
Agave durangensis	Durangensis Cenizo
Agave funkiana	Henequen Ixtle de Juarnave
Agave hookeri	Ixquitecatl Mezcal Bravo
Agave inaequidens	Raicilla
Agave karwinskii	Barril Bicuishe Cirial Largo Madrecuixe San Martinero or Sanmartín Tobaziche Tripon Verde
Agave kerchovei	Cacalia Escobeta Jabalí Pasmo
Agave lophantha	Estoquillo Mezortillo
Agave marmorata	Tepeztate

Agave maximiliana	Lechuguilla Manso Tecolote
Agave palmeri	Chino Bermejo Mano Largo
Agave pasmo	Pasmo Pasmo y Cuela
Agave pelona	Pelón Verde
Agave potatorum	Tobalá
Agave rhodacantha	Cuixe Dobadaan Mexicano Mexicano Amarillo
Agave salmiana subsp. crassispina	Salmiana
Agave scabra	Bruto De Carro Serrano
Agave seemanniana	Maguey Chato
Agave shrevei	Mahi Totosa Bacanora Ceniza
Agave tequilana	Blue Agave
Agave univittata	Estoquillo Mezortillo
Agave weberi Cels ex Poiss. (also called *Agave weberi cela*)	Maguey de Mezcal

As you can see, numerous agave varieties are suitable for making mezcal. One of the best ways to determine which ones to choose is to head down to your nearest watering hole and taste different mezcals to get an idea of their flavor profiles. The labels usually mention which agave varieties were used. Bear in mind that the results of your planting are unlikely to precisely emulate the taste of your model mezcal due to differences in your terroir, overall local conditions, and how you choose to make your spirit. It is impossible to perfectly replicate someone else's mezcal, but it is entirely doable for you to create your own unique mezcal, and your mezcal can be superb!

PROPAGATING AGAVES

There are several ways to get your agave plantings started—you can either grow them from seeds, pups, or bulbils, or you can buy bare root plants.

Growing From Seed

If you are collecting seeds or harvesting pups or bulbils from wild plants, don't harvest everything. Apply your common sense and take only what you need. This will ensure that native agaves continue to persist in the wild. Before you embark on this course of action, remember my earlier exhortation and check whether your country or state laws allow you to do this and always ask the permission of landowners if you wish to harvest these resources from plants growing on their lands. It is not simply a legal requirement, it's also good manners and fosters neighborly friendships. You might even be able to enjoy a copita of mezcal together! If you're feeling less adventurous, you can simply obtain the seeds from a nursery or seed company specializing in native plants.

An agave in full flower is an amazing sight. The flowers sometimes last for a few weeks or even months, depending on the species. Unfortunately, the plant uses so many resources to perform this marvel and set seed that it ultimately dies once the flower stem declines. The blooms develop seed pods, which eventually fall off the flower stalk, and you can collect them when this happens.

Agave seeds are flat and triangular-shaped. If the seed pod opens naturally, the seeds will be mature and black. Their size depends on the variety of agave you are growing. As with most plants, the best time to plant the seeds is at the beginning of spring. Fill pots or seed-starting flats with organic potting soil formulated specially for growing succulents. Alternatively, you can use a mixture of one part *perlite* or sand to one part compost or coconut *coir*. Sterilize the soil medium by baking it in the oven on a baking sheet on medium-low heat (350 °F or 180 °C) for about ten to fifteen minutes (Spicer, 2023). Containers must be clean and drain well. Avoid using deep pots.

Fill the pots with soil and distribute the seeds on top, about 1/2–1 inch (1–2 centimeters) apart. Scatter a thin layer of sand over them so they don't blow away, as they are very light. Don't bury them too deeply, however, as the emerging seedlings need some light to germinate and many will fail to push through. Water the flats or pots from the bottom rather than the top so that the seeds can be lightly irrigated by capillary action of the soil medium. Remove the flat or pot from the water as soon as the surface feels damp. Do this about once or twice a week depending on how quickly the soil dries out (Spicer, 2023).

Cover the pots or tray with plastic wrap or place them in a humidity dome. Keep them in a place where overnight temperatures will be between 65 °F and 75 °F (18 °C and 23 °C). You can also place the tray or pots on a heat mat set to 70 °F–75 °F (21 °C–23 °C), as this will aid germination. If you want to avoid having to harden off the plants, you can place the pots or flats outside in a sheltered spot. The seeds will germinate in about three to four weeks (Spicer, 2023).

After two months, you can feed the small plants with diluted liquid plant food. Once they have developed three true leaves, which will take about four to six months, you can place them in direct sunlight. Move the plants into the shade after a few hours and gradually increase the length of time they are exposed to the sun to harden them off (Spicer, 2023).

Growing Pups or Bulbils

An easier method of propagating agaves is to look for pups at the base of larger plants. Agaves send out runners as they age, and new plants develop on the ends of these. You can dig these pups out carefully so as not to damage the roots once they have three to four leaves (Spicer, 2023). Remember to wear thick gloves while you do this. Grasp the pup firmly, being careful not to damage the young leaves. Gently pull the plant upward. If it resists, use a trowel to loosen the soil and expose the pup's roots. Use garden shears to cut the pup off the runner if it is still attached. You can then transplant it into the ground in its final location.

Bulbils usually develop on the flower stems of mature agaves. They often fall off and self-seed. If they have developed aerial roots, you can collect them and plant them directly in the garden where you want them. If they don't have roots, then plant them in pots with suitable, sterilized potting soil. Make sure that the pots receive full sun for eight hours a day. The root systems may take several weeks or even a few months to develop. Transplant the agaves when they are 3–4 inches (6–8 centimeters) high (Spicer, 2023).

Sourcing Agaves at Plant Nurseries

If you want to buy agaves at a nursery, try to obtain bare root plants. This will enable you to check that the root system is healthy and free of fungal infections and diseases. This means you will also avoid transplanting diseases, insect larvae and eggs, or weed seeds. You can plant your bare root plants directly into healthy soil in your garden or into pots for later relocation. After planting, water them well. Thereafter, give your new agaves about an inch of water a week until they are established (Spicer, 2023).

PLANTING YOUR AGAVES

Whether you have grown your agaves from seed, sourced pups or bulbils, or purchased bare root plants from a nursery, you'll need to know from the start what their final location will be because once they are in the ground they cannot easily be replanted. Since they are arid region plants, they do best in sandy, well-drained soils and are hardy in USDA Zones 5–11. They prefer to grow in full sun and warm temperatures—between 55 °F (12.7 °C) and 100 °F (37.7 °C)—and need about eight sun hours a day (Moody Blooms, 2021).

Agaves need plenty of room to grow, so check your spacing! Consult the seed packets or other resources to understand the eventual dimensions of the variety you have selected. Measure your area and mark where each plant will be placed. It is very important to space agave correctly when they are put in the ground as their final width could reach up to 10 feet, depending on the variety (Moody Blooms, 2021). Plant them at a slight angle to facilitate drainage. If your property has a natural slope, so much the better. You can also place flat rocks or flagstones around the plant; this will aid drainage and prevent weed growth, as weeding around these thorny plants is a delicate task.

If your region experiences temperatures of over 80 °F (27 °C) for most of the day, you can site the plants in partial shade. Dig a small hole that will accommodate the root of each seedling and plant it as you would any other seedling. This means carefully turning over the pot so that the seedling is upside down and the soil is held in place by the palm of your hand. Using both hands to keep the soil around the roots, gently place the seedling into a small hole and fill the space around the transplant with *topsoil* or mature compost. Water your agaves well after planting to get them off to a good start (Spicer, 2023).

CARING FOR YOUR AGAVES

While you dream of mezcal and wait for the plants to mature, you can enjoy their development. They make a great landscaping option, as they are wonderful ornamental plants that also ensure your privacy and protection once they are larger. They need little care and grow extremely slowly, which accounts for their common name of *century plant*. Species that are heat and drought-tolerant can be planted in the ground and pretty much left to their own devices. This is the perfect way to cultivate them if you are in USDA Zones 8–11, experience high daytime temperatures, and have an arid or semiarid climate.

Besides providing you with the opportunity to make your own mezcal, agaves are low maintenance, requiring little water or fertilizer. This makes them drought-resistant and ideal for water-wise or *xeriscaped* gardens. They are also fire-resistant and especially desirable in fire-prone areas; they can protect your home and other structures from destruction. These sturdy plants are even pollinator-friendly, offering a welcome mat for native bees and butterflies. Finally, their thorny leaves dissuade deer and rabbits from snacking on them.

Once established, agaves only need watering two to three times a month in summer (Spicer, 2023). Thereafter, water them only when the soil is completely dry. These are drought-tolerant plants and overwatering can cause root rot and other blights. If the leaves turn yellow and wilt before turning brown, then the plants are getting too much water. Allow the ground to dry out completely before watering again.

Don't water agaves in winter. If you receive an abundance of winter rain, cover the plants with a clear plastic sheet suspended above them on a frame so they don't get too wet. If you live in an area with more than 20 inches (50 centimeters) of annual precipitation, consider planting Blue Weber agave (the variety traditionally used for tequila), as it is more water tolerant.

Although many types of agave grow in the mountains where the weather can get quite cold, they normally cannot thrive in frosty conditions. Agaves are susceptible to cold based on the combination of duration and intensity. The lower the temperature, the shorter the duration that agaves can withstand damage.

As mentioned in Chapter 1, biodegradable anti-transpirant sprays form, around vulnerable leaves, a waxy seal that dries out the stomata. It is the expansion of water volume when it becomes an ice crystal which enlarges and ultimately bursts plant cells, so minimizing water availability is directly protective to the leaf. You can purchase an anti-transpirant at your local nursery or farm supply store, and remember that the spray only works if applied before cold exposure!

Physical barriers trap warmer air near agaves, providing effective protection from both *radiation freezing* and *convection freezing*. Laying a layer of fleece on the ground beneath an agave plant slows the rate of heat radiation from the soil during the night, so that the covered soil is slightly warmer than bare soil during the coldest time of night. A layer of plastic draped over the foliage of your agaves keeps a blanket of warmer air around the plants. Plastic can reduce the rate of heat exchange between the leaves and the sky. It can also slow the rate of cooling caused by frosty air blowing on the leaves during a winter storm.

Agaves love dry and sunny days the way I loved pesto pasta as a teenager. This is especially true in winter when good *insolation* can significantly protect agave plants. Honestly, I still love pesto pasta.

Agaves don't require much fertilizer, but applying additional nutrients to the soil once a year will make the plant grow faster so it matures faster. Avoid foliar feeding your agaves once they are established, as their leaves don't absorb many of the nutrients.

If you need to remove dead or damaged leaves, wear gloves to protect yourself from the sharp spines and irritating sap. Use clean, sharp pruning shears or a knife or machete to cut away the leaves. Avoid removing leaves from the plant during winter.

PESTS AND DISEASES

Agaves are hardy plants and rarely experience pest or disease problems. One exception is the snout weevil. Snout weevils are unwelcome pests. The females bore tiny holes at the base of the stems and then lay their eggs in them. The brown grubs hatch and tend to go unnoticed until they pupate, as they live inside the plant. Signs of infestation include leaf damage near the stem, leaves that begin wilting at the bottom of the plant and subsequently higher up, or rotten areas on the core. Weevils usually arrive when the plants are getting ready to bloom, but they can be transported with the soil in nursery pots. In severe cases, the agave might fall over. The activities of the weevils also increase the agaves' susceptibility to diseases. The insects may spread to nearby plants and are difficult to control, but you and your agave are not utterly defenseless. Neem oil and insecticidal soaps generally work well to overcome the small assailants. Protection starts at planting time. If your agaves are widely spaced, weevils will have to work harder to move between plants. Relocate any pups before they are attacked. Also keep an eye out for scale insects or mealybugs. When necessary, you can use thoughtfully selected insecticides to combat these problems.

Black spot or anthracnose is a fungal disease that spreads when plants get too wet. If you see signs of the problem, you can cut off and destroy infected leaves. You can also use a copper-based fungicide if the infection is not too serious.

Crown and root rot are other fungal pathogens that are spread through water and wet soil. It is important to allow the soil to dry out completely between watering cycles to prevent root and crown rot from appearing. A natural substance that is effective against many plant pathogens is *Bacillus subtilis*, a bacteria that controls many of these disease-causing microorganisms, so look for products containing these bacteria.

If you are new to farming or gardening, you may find the last few paragraphs intimidating. Keep in mind that most other plants and crops are more susceptible than agave to infestation and disease. If you regularly survey your cultivated area, you will notice any sign of trouble and be able to respond before a small issue becomes a big one.

Now that you have discovered more about agave and found out how to propagate and grow your own plants, it's time to learn how to make your own mezcal.

CRAFTING YOUR OWN MEZCAL AT HOME

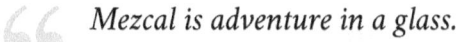

> *Mezcal is adventure in a glass.*
>
> — ALEX WHITE

> *Love speaks in flowers. Truth requires thorns.*
>
> — LEIGH BARDUGO

In this chapter, you'll learn everything you need to know about making your own mezcal at home.

Assuming you've grown or have access to suitable agaves, now's the time to harvest them in the first step to creating your own mezcal.

Some less enterprising souls might wither in trepidation and say, "Don't try this at home!" You have come this far and your friends have been waiting. The time has come to harness your adventurous spirits and launch the harvest operation.

BEFORE YOU START

At the end of this chapter, you will find a shopping list of agave-harvesting and mezcal-making items. Worry not! You can get most of these items as you go.

Before you harvest the piñas from your agave plants, you will need to make some preparations.

The first step is to dig a large pit for roasting your harvested agave piñas. Find a suitable spot in your garden and commence the excavation. Make sure that it is roomy enough to contain the piñas, together with the wood, coals, and covering you will use for the fire. Line the pit with large rocks on which to place the piñas. To give you an idea, commercial mezcaleros aim for a pit which can hold around seven tons of material (Doochin, 2015). Picture something 10–15 feet (3–5 meters) across and 3–6 feet (1–2 meters) deep. Considering the depth and breadth of the maw you'll be etching into the local topography, it might be wise to rent a backhoe or invite your friends to bring their shovels. If you encounter hardpan, you will appreciate more aggressive tools like picks and mattocks. Don't worry about making the pit too big!

It's always wise to begin an endeavor with the end in mind. If your community has a Homeowner's Association (HOA), consider whether your residential lot might be the prime subject of the next meeting before you break ground.

Somewhere near the roasting pit, a large, preferably cemented area will also be required. You will need to break up and smash the agave piñas on this surface once the roasting is finished. Another option is to invest in some plastic cement-mixing trays. Regardless of the surface, every anvil invites a mallet. You can use something like a baseball bat or wooden posts to crush the agave by hand.

You will also need a rain barrel or similar vat that can hold around 350 gallons (1,000 liters) of liquid (Doochin, 2015). Smaller alternatives are large glass carboys or stainless steel pots, although their capacity is limited. Whichever receptacle you select, remember to allow extra space for the agave mush.

Finally, you will need a still. You can purchase copper alembic and stainless steel stills from online retailers or distillery suppliers.

Harvesting the Piñas

When selecting piñas to harvest for mezcal-making, focus on your biggest, oldest plants, as their swollen stems will contain the most sugars. If you leave the roots in the ground, the sweet sap will often continue to flow for several hours. This sap can also be collected and added to your mezcal during fermentation and distillation.

Piñas are best harvested in spring or fall, when the plant is still actively growing, and preferably on a cool day. This will also make the process more comfortable. You are probably not a well-conditioned professional jimador, and harvesting a plant that is an average of five to eight feet tall and seven to twelve feet in diameter will probably seem rather daunting (Agave Harvesting, n.d.).

I know what you're thinking. It's advisable to call in reinforcements, so plan ahead and ask your friends and neighbors to assist. Consider making a day or weekend of it and turn the endeavor into a social occasion. Community-building activities are appreciated now more than ever, as we are living in the midst of an epidemic of loneliness. You might be surprised at how excited your neighbors are to hear from you and get to know you better. To fuel your helpers and maintain morale, consider ordering pizza or providing the type of food and refreshments that will sustain your particular group.

Ahead of time and throughout the day, you could have a dedicated photographer (this could be a friend or family member) take pictures to immortalize the event and encourage the participants to plan community-building projects of their own.

A simple handout with a checklist, job descriptions, and safety recommendations will provide guidance to each member of the harvest crew and help everyone check that everything is ready for the big day.

You will need to get your hands on a few sharp machetes, small saws, and pruning tools. Before you start, ensure that you and your assistants are wearing appropriate safety clothing. Wear safety glasses to shield your eyes from the sap and thick, sturdy gloves to protect your hands from the thorns. It's also a good idea to sport long pants, a long-sleeved shirt, and sturdy boots.

I have learned firsthand the importance of donning suitable attire before approaching agave plants. I once bent over to help my daughter into her car seat, and inadvertently backed into the sharp spine of an agave leaf. I cried out in pain, immediately realizing my mistake, and have since developed a keener awareness of the presence of nearby cacti and thorny succulents. With this in mind, encourage your harvest crew to hold off on drinking beer until after the work is finished!

If the plants have pups that you would like to keep, remove them carefully and set them aside in a shady spot for later transplanting. Then, begin the process of harvesting the piñas. First, remove the thorns from the leaf edges and tips. Start at the bottom of the leaf, working your way to the tip. You can use a sharp, sturdy knife or a pruning tool for this. Using a machete or small saw, remove all the leaves at their bases—or as many as possible.

The idea is to expose the piña so it can be severed from the plant's roots. As the name suggests, the piña will look like a giant pineapple at the heart of the plant. Remove any spines that might still be present, as well as any pieces of leaf. Finally, use a machete, shovel, or garden fork to separate the bottom of the piña from the roots. Once severed, pull the piña toward you to remove it from the remainder of the plant. This is not going to be an easy task, as the average piña can weigh anywhere from 80–200 pounds (36–90 kilograms) (Agave Harvesting, n.d.). You'll need all the help you can get. After this, you can cut up the piñas and move them to your fire pit. If you are on a large lot, you might need to transport them in someone's truck.

You can put the leaves into your compost heap to decompose naturally, but if you wish to experience a little bit of what life could have been like for an ancient Aztec desirous to make use of every little bit of the earth's resources, you can eat the cooked agave leaves and the remains of the flower stalk. The leaves are very fibrous, so choose your portion size wisely. The leaves are toxic to humans, so refrain from eating them raw. The raw leaves are moderately poisonous and contain an acrid essential oil, as well as oxalic acid and oxalates in concentrations that can lead to kidney stones. The foliage also contains a toxic hemolytic sapogenin and bitter-tasting *saponins*, which are soap-like substances.

There are indications, however, that certain saponins may accelerate renal clearance of oxalates, which implies a pleasing chemical balance in the agave leaf. Green tea, raspberry, pomegranate, and parsley contain saponins and other compounds which inhibit crystal formation in the human bladder (Nirumand et al, 2018).

Another study concluded that saponins extracted from Hairy Rupturewort (a desert succulent), are an effective treatment for kidney stones (Fouada et al, 2006). I find it utterly fascinating that the antidote to a toxic desert succulent is found in another desert succulent!

At your post-harvest celebration, make sure that you cook the agave thoroughly to break down its toxins. As with rhubarb, boiling removes most of the oxalates from agave leaves. The heat also breaks down the bitter saponins to make the leaves more palatable. Your cooked leaves may be safe to eat, but will they delight the palate? Perhaps you can limit yourself to preparing a very small cooked-leaf serving for each of your guests. As the saying goes, they can always ask for seconds. You can even have a themed door prize for those who actually sample more of the dish!

Roasting

Cut the piñas into quarters or slightly smaller pieces using an ax or machete. Start the fire in your pit, using wood that is available locally, such as oak, mesquite, or even eucalyptus. Remember that the flavors the wood confers will enter your mezcal. When the fire has burned down to coals, you can lay your piña pieces on the stones around the pit. Cover them with palm fronds or other similar garden waste and sand in alternating layers. Aim for a cone shape with the fire in the center. Cover the entire assembly with a wet canvas tarp and layer more sand on top of it. If you prefer to avoid the specter of your county, commune, or borough fire inspector standing with a scowl at the back gate to your house, be sure to research the need for a local burn permit before you roast. These are usually reserved at least a few days beforehand, so it's prudent to check on this well in advance. Each jurisdiction has its own rules, and the regulations are often seasonal.

Milling

Your piñas should be ready after four to five days of roasting (Doochin, 2015). Remove the coverings from the fire and take out your piñas. They should be fibrous and sweet to the taste. Bring the roasted piñas to the area where you are going to smash them and beat them to a pulp. You can use baseball bats, heavy timbers, or other suitable equipment. This job obviously requires heavy-duty gloves. Be prepared to spend several days doing the milling. It's a tremendous natural boost to your cardiovascular fitness!

Collect the fibers and nectar as you go and place them in the large barrel or vat. This container should be located in a warm place affording some protection from the elements, such as under a covered roof. When you're finished, the agave fiber and nectar mix will have the appearance of rich pond mud. Don't let it frighten you! Time and love will eventually convert it to clear mezcal.

Fermentation

Fermentation is a biological process caused by the action of yeasts. Yeasts are single-celled organisms that reproduce prolifically in the high-sugar environment of the fermentation vat, feeding on the simple sugars, such as fructose and glucose, that are present. Yeasts convert these sugars into alcohol and release carbon dioxide as a natural byproduct. For this process to be effective, ambient air temperatures need to be around 82.4 °F (28 °C). Mezcal is fermented in wooden vats if naturally occurring yeasts are used or in bio-fermenters if commercial yeasts are to be added.

You can also use fermentation equipment employed in winemaking, such as carboys or even large plastic buckets equipped with airlocks. If you wish to have more control over the fermentation process, the mixture needs to be enriched with nitrogen in the form of ammonium sulfate and one of the *Saccharomyces cerevisiae* yeasts. Yeast selection depends on the species or variety of agave that was harvested. A good champagne yeast such as Lalvin EC-1118 can also be effective (Scarlet, 2020; Francesco et al., 2012). The actions of these yeasts also greatly influence the aromas of mezcal.

Because it takes such a long time to pound all the agave fiber, fermentation will already have started by the time it's all in the barrel. You can add some good quality, chlorine-free water at this point. Yeast and chlorine don't get along well. Do not fill the tank too full, as the contents will bubble and expand during the fermentation process due to the release of carbon dioxide. Allow plenty of space to avoid losing some of your ferment on the ground. Temperatures during fermentation should ideally be between 77 °F and 86 °F (25 °C and 30 °C) (Francisco et al., 2012).

Fermentation is often complete within seven days, once the sugars have been exhausted. Keep an eye on your fermentation. When the mixture has stopped bubbling and the liquid no longer tastes sweet, you can begin the distillation process. Before doing so, use an instrument called a hydrometer to measure the alcohol content (ABV) of your mixture. Hydrometers can be obtained online or at wine shops (Scarlet, 2020).

Once fermentation is completed, all the solids must be strained out of the liquid before it is distilled. The easiest way to do this is to strain the alcoholic liquid through cheesecloth. You can use an easy siphon to empty your barrel. Collect the resulting liquid in stainless steel pots.

Distillation

This is the final step in your mezcal-making process, and it's probably the most important. Distillation is the method used to separate the alcohol and water, which is possible because they reach their boiling point at different temperatures—ethanol (alcohol) boils at a lower temperature than water. As the alcohol vapor and aromatics contact the cool surface of the condenser coil, they return to liquid form. Every drop of mezcal you enjoy was in a gaseous state at one point in time!

Distillation determines the alcohol content of the mezcal. The official Mexican standard (Marina, 2017) for mezcal-making puts this at between 35% and 45% ABV at a temperature of 68 °F (20 °C). The ABV influences the aromas and flavors of mezcal, as well as their intensity and the smoothness of the drink. It's important to arrive at the correct ABV after distillation. Too high and the mezcal will be too strong with unbalanced flavors. Too low and it will be poorly flavored and watery. The ideal alcohol level for unaged joven mezcal, for example, usually averages between 40% and 55%, but this varies somewhat depending on the preference of the mezcalero (Montero, 2024).

To distill your mezcal, you will need (Doran, 2023):

- pot still
- still burner
- hydrometer
- easy siphon
- cleaning products

Assemble the still according to the manufacturer's instructions. Check that all the clamps, domes, condensers, and piping are tight and that everything is correctly installed.

Before you start, it's essential to clean out your still (if you don't, you could end up with a sub-standard mezcal after all your efforts). To do this, allow 4–5 gallons (15–19 liters) of water to run through the still for about three to four hours (Doran, 2023). After this, transfer your fermented agave liquid into the still. It's best to use a siphon to keep excessive sediment from entering your distillation, as it could ruin an otherwise good batch of mezcal.

If you're a closet pyromaniac like my childhood friend Pedrito, I know you're just itching to light the burner and start distilling! Before you flick your lighter, keep a few safety tips in mind. Even if your still is well-sealed, alcohol vapor can escape from the condenser coil. It is important to only light your burner in a thoroughly ventilated outdoor area, as carbon monoxide, alcohol vapor, fire, and you don't mix. Don heat-resistant gloves and safety glasses, and don't allow any horseplay around your still. Mezcal-making is serious business!

Now it's time to fire up the still. If you are using a condenser, turn on the water when the boiler temperature reaches 130 °F (54.4 °C). The still will start producing when the temperature reaches 168 °F (75.5 °C). At that point, progressively increase the temperature to continue receiving distillate. Monitor the alcohol level and stop the distillation when it reaches 20% ABV. Retain the distillate for the second distillation. Measure the amount of spirit collected and dilute it by adding 20% water. Stir the mixture thoroughly and return it to the still. Add any flavorings, such as herbs, chilies, or fruits, and begin your second distillation (Doran, 2023). Follow the same process as for the first one. When it is finished, you can collect your mezcal.

When the second distillation is complete, you can do a taste test and see which different flavors you can identify. Pour your mezcal into glass bottles. The alcohol content will still be extremely high. Let the spirit age in the bottles for eighty days before blending your mezcal with water to reduce the alcohol content. Aim for around 44%–45% ABV (Scarlet, 2020).

AGING YOUR MEZCAL

You can age your mezcals in glass—and many mezcaleros do, as mentioned previously—but if you wish to age your mezcal to produce distinctive flavors, the best strategy is to rely on barrels.

Although French and oak barrels are usually preferred, other woods, including acacia, cherry, chestnut, guayacan wood, and pine can all be used. Even oak barrels come in several variants, including aged, toasted, and smoked. Aging mezcal is usually a slow process that ultimately softens the flavor and often produces a darker color. This is because tannins and flavonoids naturally present in the wood are released into the mezcal during aging. You will need to be patient, as time is what gives these elixirs their uniqueness and special flavor. One of the captivating aspects of mezcal is that you must wait patiently for it to be ready. In a world of on-demand services, home delivery, and skippable online advertisements, we have grown accustomed to quick results and quick dopamine hits. Some of the most important things in life, though, cannot be rushed. Greatness in marriage, in children, and in a great many academic and skilled pursuits takes time. Championship golfers, master surgeons, and virtuosic pianists all understand the necessity of investing years of focused effort to achieve excellence. Mezcal rewards the patient, and you may even learn something about yourself as your batches of the spirit quietly age.

The long preparations and thoughtful waiting also connect us to our own ancestral cultures, no matter their origin. Our forebears did not get their supplies from well-provisioned local stores. If they needed barrels, they ordered them from a cooper and waited patiently. If there was no cooper or if they couldn't afford his services, they simply had to make their own barrels. Waiting for mezcal to age allows us to experience a little history and develop a new appreciation for those who came before us.

While mezcal is not always aged in barrels, there is increasing demand for aged spirits among aficionados. To create a reposado, the mezcal needs to be aged for at least two months, an añejo for at least twelve months, and an extra añejo for a minimum of thirty-six months (Resendiz, 2023).

There are three stages of aging (Resendiz, 2023):

State	Time	Process
Extraction Stage	6–12 months	All flavors and aromas of the wood are extracted and enter the distillate.
Stabilization Stage	12–24 months	The flavors stabilize.
Aging Stage	24–36 months (or more)	The flavors and aromas become smooth and integrated, giving the mezcal body and character.

The type of mezcal you wish to make will determine how long you choose to age it. Mezcal can be stored in oak barrels for anywhere from fourteen months to three years (Francesco et al., 2012).

Ensure that the barrels are in good condition and meticulously washed between distillations. Partially fill the empty barrels with water before adding stones and swishing them around to remove any undesirable elements from the inside of the barrel. Barrels are usually filled with water when not in use so the wood doesn't dry out and they don't crack or split.

In the next chapter, you'll find out more about how to enhance the flavor profiles of your mezcal to personalize your spirit and make it truly unique.

Mezcal-Making Shopping List

Here is a shopping list of agave-harvesting and mezcal-making items:

- backhoe and digging tools
- plastic cement-mixing trays (if you lack a cemented area near the roasting pit)

- large rocks
- baseball bat or wooden posts
- rain barrel or large glass carboys or stainless steel pots
- large plastic buckets with airlocks
- machetes, saws, and pruning tools
- sturdy work gloves
- gloves insulated for high temperatures
- safety glasses
- fire extinguisher
- friends, pizza, and cold beverages
- large canvas tarp
- sand
- ammonium sulfate
- yeast
- flavorings, if you desire to infuse chilies, herbs, or fruits
- pot still (could be stainless steel or copper alembic)
- still burner
- hydrometer
- easy siphon
- cleaning products
- glass bottles

CUSTOMIZING AND
EXPERIMENTING WITH MEZCAL

> *Todo acto de creación es un acto de amor.*
>
> *Every act of creation is an act of love.*
>
> — JOSÉ REVUELTAS

> *Let's see what this button does.*
>
> — MY BROTHER

Now that you know how to make your own mezcal, it's time to discover how to personalize your efforts so you can create flavor profiles that will make your creations unique and special.

When crafting your own spirit, regardless of where you are, you can be faithful to the spirit of the traditional process by using products that are local to your own area. One of the magnificent aspects of mezcal creation is that it is largely individualized; you can boast about your local novelty the way many artisans proudly display objects they carefully fashioned from locally sourced items.

FLAVOR CUSTOMIZATION TECHNIQUES

When mezcaleros use earthen pits and local traditional methods, the roasting process creates the spirit's signature smoky aromas and taste. The sugars in the agaves caramelize, adding their sweet richness to the flavor profile. When the piñas are roasted in above-ground pits or stainless steel ovens, the resulting mezcal acquires a non-traditional taste. During artisanal or ancestral mezcal production, no commercial yeasts are added to fermentation vats—this is prohibited when ancestral mezcal is produced. The mezcal fibers and water are collected in a barrel and allowed to ferment in the open air. As mentioned previously, this brings them into contact with all the wild yeasts that are naturally present in the environment. This causes every batch of mezcal slightly different, even when it's made by the same mezcalero using the same agave varieties harvested in the same area. The yeasts vary according to the prevailing environmental conditions, creating a naturally capricious product, which is one of mezcal's charms.

The type of still also affects the flavor of the end product. Today, most artisanal and traditional mezcal producers use copper stills because they are more efficient, and larger batches can be distilled at one time. Another benefit to using these stills is that the copper leaches out the sulfate compounds, which helps to make the mezcal lighter and gives it a crisper taste. Distilling mezcal in clay tends to confer bolder, more earthy flavors. In both cases, the heat required for distillation is usually generated by a fire.

However, utilizing modern column stills produces a different type of mezcal. On the one hand, it gives rise to much purer forms of alcohol. On the other hand, its resulting flavors and textures are less complex and much reduced, which isn't necessarily what you want when it comes to agave spirits.

INFUSING MEZCAL WITH UNIQUE FLAVORS

One of the ways to impart special flavors to your mezcal is to infuse the finished spirit with other ingredients. The prospects for experimentation are endless, and you might end up with some surprisingly great tastes and unforgettable flavors.

Spicy Infusion

Spicy infusions usually complement mezcals made from espadin or, if you're fortunate enough to obtain it, from the rarer tobalá agave. Try using two jalapeño peppers and two serrano peppers (Meghan, 2022). Don't remove the seeds, as these add extra flavor and heat. Wash and slice the peppers, then fill a mason jar with mezcal and add the peppers. Let the drink infuse the drink overnight and taste it to see whether it's to your liking. Remember that this infusion can rapidly become very hot and spicy, so it's advisable to taste it at least every twelve hours (Meghan, 2022). Strain out the peppers and seeds when you're happy with the flavor. Store the infusion in an airtight container in a cool place.

Habanero Infusion

This infusion is ideal for homemade mezcal, as long as you have 25 ounces (750 milliliters) available. To make this infusion, cut three habanero chilies in half and seed them. Add them to the mezcal. Allow them to infuse for twelve hours and then taste the drink (Claire, 2012). Once you are happy with the flavor, strain out the habaneros and enjoy.

Hibiscus Flower Infusion

For this infusion, it's important to use dried flowers and a digital scale to ensure that you use just the right amount. You will need 2 tablespoons (25 grams) of dried hibiscus flowers per 25 ounces (750 milliliters) of mezcal. Measure the flowers into a large mason jar with an airtight lid. Add the mezcal, seal the jar, and leave it to infuse for four hours (Sullivan, 2016). This will turn the mezcal bright pink. Strain the drink first through a fine mesh strainer to remove the flowers and then through a coffee filter to remove any remaining sediment. To bottle it, use a funnel.

Roasted Pineapple Infusion

Preheat the oven to 375 °F (180 °C). Remove the peel from a pineapple, slice it, and then cube the pieces. Place the chunks onto a baking sheet and bake them until lightly browned. After they have cooled, measure 12 ounces (355 milliliters) of mezcal into a mason jar and add the pineapple. Seal, shake well, and leave to stand for forty-eight hours. Then, strain the mezcal through cheesecloth. The infusion will keep in the refrigerator for up to three months (DeFilippo, 2023).

Cilantro and Lime Infusion

To make this infusion, combine 13.5 ounces (400 milliliters) of mezcal with 2.5 ounces (100 grams) of cilantro and 1 tablespoon (15 grams) of lime zest in a mason jar with a tight-fitting lid. Allow to stand for forty-eight hours, giving the jar a shake every eight to ten hours (Folsey, 2023). Thereafter, strain and enjoy.

AGING AND FLAVORS

When mezcal is matured in glass, it remains a colorless liquid, although its texture softens and it becomes more robust. The mezcal's flavors become more complex as the compounds within it interact with one another and with the spirit. This creates richness and complexity.

When mezcal is stored and aged in barrels, the flavors of the wood leach into the mezcal distillate over time. The flavor that results depends on the wood used, as different woods impart their own flavors, creating enhanced flavors and aromas. For example, American white oak barrels confer spicy, smoky, and sweet aromas and flavors, while French oak adds notes of chocolate, dried fruits, and vanilla. As soon as mezcal hits his or her palate, a connoisseur will be able to discern its approximate age and identify the type of barrel wood in which it was stored.

NUANCES IN MEZCAL BLENDS

The majority of mezcal is still artisanally or traditionally produced. This gives it its unique character, as the results depend on such variables as which agave species are available at a particular time, what the sugar content of the plants is, and how much material is used to fill the fermentation vats and stills.

In practice, agave is harvested when it is ready. You cannot exactly determine the timing beforehand, as you might for a pencil produced in a factory. Whether the producers secure the agave from the wild, from their own private fields, or from other landowners, they will be limited by the types of agave that are suitable for harvest at that time.

Sometimes, the amount of roasted agave derived from a certain species doesn't quite fill a fermentation vat, so the *palenquero* (distiller) fills it with roast agave from another species. There are times when palenqueros deliberately decide to mix certain agave species because they find that the taste of the mezcal derived from a particular combination is particularly good. This practice is reminiscent of wine blending. At other times, a distillery might want to marry a high-sugar agave with a low-sugar one to create a mezcal that's neither too sweet nor too dry. This might also mean that more mezcal can be produced from one batch with fewer plants.

Ensemble

Sometimes, mezcaleros select agaves based on availability. At other times, they remember a successful blending experiment or rely on proprietary or family knowledge about an exceptional blend. Blend, of course, is wine parlance. Successful winemakers combine different grapes to create a certain type of wine. When it comes to mezcal, this is often referred to as an *ensemble*, which essentially means that the final product is a field blend. Producing mezcal from several types of agaves, all of which might have different sizes, roasting times, and fermentation and distilling requirements, can be complex, but the ability to balance these variables enables producers to create unusual mezcals. No matter how splendid, these mezcals may be unique. If you are sampling one, remember that the very distinctive spirit you are tasting may never be exactly replicated again.

Mezcal producers' choice of the term *ensemble* elevates their spirits to new heights. The word *ensemble* means "together" in French. It is often used in a musical context to describe musicians who strive to create a harmonious, complementary, and concerted sound. The loveliness of the aesthetics and the complexity of the music awaken strong emotions, a physical response, and intellectual engagement in the listener. An outstanding mezcal ensemble may awaken some of these in a connoisseur.

Mezcla

Mezcla is the Spanish word for "mixture". It is not the same as an *ensemble*. Mezcla mezcals are a combination of different batches of mezcal made at different times and from various agave species. The mezcalero might take a batch of espadin-based mezcal and mix it with a batch produced using *Agave americano,* for example. Achieving exactly the right blend is something of an art, and it often results in unusual and special mezcals.

Producers sometimes create mezclas to deliver a more cost-effective mezcal, combining a rarer agave species with a more common one, such as espadin, in such a way that the mezcal retains the characteristics and flavor profiles of the more costly product without the high price tag. Similarly, my wedding ring is principally comprised of palladium. The shine is just as true as that of a pure gold ring, and the love expressed is just as strong!

Blend

Blending is often linked to industrial mezcal production. Several large-scale, factory-style distilleries can purchase large quantities of mezcal from different sources and combine them. The result, obviously, is a blend. Alternatively, a smaller distillery can produce a wide variety of batches, which are then blended together. These blends are easily distinguishable one from the other.

Essentially, the difference between these three mixing styles (ensemble, mezcla, and blending) is that the mixing occurs at the beginning of production in an ensemble, whereas it takes place after distillation when it comes to a mezcla or blend. To avoid confusion for drinkers and buyers outside of Mexico, labels on mezcal bottles often simply refer to an ensemble, which can include any of these three processes. Colloquial words like *mezcla* are also not as broadly understood as ensemble.

Mixing Your Mezcal

After you've produced a few mezcals of your own, you can try your hand at blending. You may want to get creative with the mezcals you have already made, and like big-name brands, experiment with adding other ingredients to them or combining them with other alcoholic beverages.

Unlike tequila, mezcals—with their bold, strong, smoky flavors—are unlikely to be overpowered by most mixers. On the face of it, the complex, earthy flavors of mezcal make it surprisingly versatile when mixed with other ingredients. While cocktails generally combine mezcal with fruit and fruit juices, mezcal can also be mixed with other spirits, such as amaro, vermouth, and different types of bitters. You might even want to add your own beverage of choice to a mezcal purchased at your favorite liquor store.

Each batch of mezcal will be slightly different from the next because of the artisanal way most mezcals are made. This will apply to your homemade spirits as well. Mixing your mezcals with other ingredients or even combining different ones will therefore create something unique. Start small, tasting and taking notes as you go until the desired result is achieved. Depending how much of a certain blend you want to make, you can scale up your recipe. You can even combine your mezcal with tequila for a different taste experience.

When it comes to creating mezcal-based drinks, the possibilities are endless. Mixing other beverages with mezcal can be exciting and interesting. Experiment with different flavors, infusions, and mixes until you achieve something unique and special. You can enjoy these yourself, showcase them at dinner parties, or give them away as unusual gifts.

I hope that over the course of this book, you have acquired fresh knowledge about mezcal, the variegated and venerable beverage once consumed only in the Mexican hinterlands, that's now rapidly becoming mainstream across the globe. You've found out about the agaves used to make it and about the process of mezcal production, as well as how to pair it with Mexican foods and create mezcal-based cocktails. You've also learned how to grow your own agaves and make mezcal on your own property.

You might have heard rumors about the soaring popularity of mezcal and the impact it has had on agave growers. In the next chapter, we will explore the trajectory and likely future of this singular alcoholic beverage.

THE FUTURE OF MEZCAL

> *Mezcal is so simple, yet so complicated.*
>
> — SUSAN COSS

> *The most powerful warriors are patience and time.*
>
> — LEO TOLSTOY

Stoked by the ever-increasing international demand for agave spirits, the mezcal industry is poised for expansion. How will this affect the artisanal nature of mezcal, producers in quiet country enclaves, and the availability of agave? In this chapter, you'll discover more about the challenges facing the industry and learn about some of the innovative solutions that have already begun to solve them.

CURRENT TRENDS AND FUTURE PREDICTIONS

Not long after tequila became mainstream and sought-after, mezcal—its smoky country cousin—started taking the market by storm (BevAlc Insights Team, 2022). Mezcal's appeal lies in its handcrafted uniqueness and artisanal nature. If consumed with wisdom and moderation, it's also considered a healthy drink due in part to its low glycemic index of just 10%–14% on average, as well as to its plant-based nature (Mordor Intelligence, 2023). Another trend contributing to mezcal's popularity is the propensity of buyers to try out new and unusual premium products.

Most mezcal drinkers are millennials in their late 20s to early 40s (BevAlc Insights Team, 2022). This group's higher disposable income has helped to drive sales, despite slightly higher price points for mezcal when compared to other spirits. While there is certainly interest in mezcal in other demographics, older drinkers have been slower to embrace it.

Because of its proximity to Mexico, the United States remains the largest international market for mezcal, accounting for around 50% of its international market share. However, with the increasing popularity of cocktails—which is how many drinkers first experience mezcal—both the United States and emerging markets such as China and India have seen higher demand. Japan has been importing mezcal for some time, and there has also been considerable interest in Australia. Producers have begun offering more choices and innovative flavors, enabling consumers to fully appreciate mezcal's uniqueness. As incomes have risen across Asia, demand for innovative, premium, and luxury spirits has followed. Aged reposado mezcal is particularly popular, as the maturation process creates a smoother, more full-bodied drink while conferring vanilla, caramel, and woody flavors.

In 2023, mezcal's global market share was valued at $960.4 million, and it is expected to increase at a 12.36% compound annual growth rate (CAGR) to over a billion dollars by 2029. Europe is anticipated to be the fastest-growing market in the future (Mordor Intelligence, 2023).

MAINTAINING AUTHENTICITY IN A GLOBAL MARKETPLACE

Not long ago, mezcal-making was limited to an age-old family tradition. The spirit was produced in relatively small quantities in backyards and on isolated farms for local enjoyment. Its consumption marked special occasions—engagements, weddings, the birth of a baby, or coming-of-age celebrations. It was drunk at festivals and funerals, and offered to the deceased. Sometimes, it was used medicinally, rubbed on aching feet, or taken to relieve stomach ailments.

The agaves to make it grew abundantly and were harvested as required, while local forests provided firewood for roasting and distilling. Both the huge agaves and the necessary firewood were transported to rudimentary distilleries using donkeys and rickety carts. Roasting, fermenting, distilling, and flavoring the spirit was a family affair, where even children were roped in to keep horses or donkeys turning the big stone tahonas. Distilleries were primitive by today's standards, often little more than a converted barn or a small setup in an urban outbuilding, using equipment that was frequently handed down from grandfather to father to son.

That was before the mezcal craze hit North America and the rest of the world. Many were already familiar with mezcal's cousin, tequila, another agave spirit steeped in Mexican culture. Skyrocketing demand for tequila resulted in the greater industrialization of its manufacture. Much tequila is now mass-produced in factories using modern autoclaves, stainless steel vats, commercial yeasts, and column distilleries. From these polished assembly lines emerge ample stocks of product for distributors to ship across the world. A big question in the mezcal-producing regions of Mexico today is: Is mezcal destined for the same fate?

Like tequila, demand for mezcal is exploding, with stocks selling out almost as fast as the spirit can be made. By 2020, Mexican production had increased by 400%. For distilleries, this can translate to significant volumes. To safeguard production quality and maintain fidelity to tradition, the Mexican government developed regulations for the industry in 1994, including a provision that mezcal had to be made with 100% agave. Certification has become prohibitively expensive for some, costing anywhere from $375 to $2,500 annually (Osigwe, 2023). In addition, denomination of origin (DO) rules have made it difficult for some producers to retain their traditional production methods. This has led a number of family-owned brands to abandon certification in the interest of maintaining their historic mezcal-making customs. Corruption allegations, always a concern, have further tarnished the certification's reputation. Corruption must be reined in to protect this and every other industry and human endeavor.

In addition, certification has made it easier for large, international corporations to swoop in, dominating the agave spirits landscape. As can be expected, high demand has inevitably generated competition, but what most consumers don't know is that many of their favorite brands aren't actually Mexican-owned. For example, El Silencio is owned by New Yorkers, Del Maguey has French owners, and Casamigos is British. Many such companies don't produce mezcal themselves but buy significant quantities from Mexican producers, rebranding and then selling it at premium prices. Traditional producers are often sidelined, generally seeing only a fraction of this income.

Small, traditional mezcal producers are being squeezed between certification and better financial returns or the maintenance of their cultural traditions. A literal Mexican standoff has ensued, and it's not yet clear what the outcome will be.

However, big brands that take a lion share of the proceeds offer in return access to retail distribution channels and brand name recognition at the point of sale. They are providing value, otherwise there would be no exchange. In many cases, small and part-time family businesses have seen their economic situation dramatically improve when investors propelled their obscure mezcal from their village plastic-jug distribution venture to sudden international exposure. Even when investors demand a high price for their contribution, the financial benefits to the original producers and their community outweigh the option of remaining in obscurity.

AGAVE AVAILABILITY: A THORNY QUESTION

The dramatic increase in demand for agave spirits obviously impacts producers' interest in securing additional agave plants. They have turned their attention to wild species growing in previously unharvested areas farther into the countryside. At the same time, scientifically-designed agave plantations, able to generate up to ten times as much agave than uncultivated fields on the same amount of land, continue to expand and create opportunities for new growers.

Parts of Mexico include community-owned lands called *ejido* that determine access to agricultural land. In prime agave areas, growers select the succulents to plant on their individual parcels.

Since prices for agave have risen exponentially, small farmers who have access to ejido land are easily able to find a buyer for their crop. Additionally, buyers are willing to pay more than ever before. This is true even for agriculture on a very limited scale. It makes more sense for small farmers to focus on agave than on other crops.

Sustainable use means wisely harvesting natural resources so they don't become depleted and are available for future generations. This certainly applies to the agaves that are used for mezcal. Of course, no one cares more about this than the people whose income and family sustenance come from the harvesting of agave or the production and sale of mezcal. This is evident in the already mentioned mezcal producers who plant two or even three agaves for each one they harvest, as do tomato farmers when they replant tomatoes after each harvest.

One common way of starting a discussion on the importance of sustainably harvesting wild agaves—or their seeds, bulbils, and pups—is to find out just how much agave it takes to make a 33.8-

ounce (1-liter) bottle of mezcal. This depends to some degree on the agave used, as well as on how big the fermentation tanks are, so the information presented below is of necessity a general guideline.

As with fine wine, there is a massive premium for ancestral spirits, since they entail more exacting production protocols and offer a rarefied gastronomic experience.

With a rarer agave variety such as tepextate, it can take an astonishing 12,866 pounds (1,300 kilograms) of agave to make 101.4 ounces (3 liters) of spirit. Part of the reason is that this type of agave takes an incredibly long time to reach optimal ripeness. This means that the sugars have had plenty of time to develop and become complex, resulting in a mezcal with intense and complex flavors. Espadin, on the other hand, takes only four years to mature to the point where it can be harvested. Espadin plants also contain far more sugars than tepextate, requiring only 44–55 pounds (10–25 kilograms) of agave to produce 33.8 ounces (1 liter) of spirit (Bank & Peribán, 2020).

MAKING MEZCAL SUSTAINABLY

Agaves are grown in monoculture-style plantations to meet rising demand. In this orderly setting, the pups of larger plants are easily separated, transported, and cultivated. A common practice is to plant pups from different areas as this secures the continuation of many varieties and assures genetic diversity, which will deliver stronger and more resilient plants in the future.

Monoculture-style plantations result in more efficient land use. As seen above, many agave plantations have a plant density per acre that is ten times that found in the wild, and the plants grown with these production methods can reach more than three times the size of their wild counterparts, translating into higher yields. This generates increased revenues for farmers and reduces the pressure on wild agave populations.

In some areas, family cooperatives are semi-cultivating naturally occurring agaves to retain species that not only form an integral part of local ecosystems but also are important for mezcal production. Local growers are committed to planting more agave to replace what is harvested. This is excellent stewardship of the plants and of the land.

These sustainable practices create local jobs and preserve the cultural heritage that has thrived in these arid lands for hundreds of years. Many growers support projects where seeds are germinated in seedbeds for later transplanting into the wild. One brand even launched a portfolio of mezcals based on espadin varieties grown in this way by different communities across the Oaxacan region. Some producers have adopted a policy of planting two or even three agaves for every wild one harvested.

Polyculture techniques ensure that native biodiversity and soil quality improve as a result of agave cultivation. Seeds are sourced locally. Some producers allow a certain proportion of their plants to send up flower stalks and set seed, ensuring that the semi-cultivated plants are genetically diverse. This also feeds pollinators that utilize agave flowers. High demand for agave seed ensures a wide variety of propagation methods, including growing agaves from pups or bulbils.

Preserving and propagating the succulent may yield benefits we can little imagine today. Growers have long known that agave has many uses. In the Mexican state of Puebla in 1864, two brothers who grew agave on their land and carefully researched it recorded the following in their groundbreaking book titled Memoria Sobre el Maguey Mexicano (Agave Maximilianea) [Monograph on the

Mexican Maguey (Agave Maximilianea)] (Blasquez and Blasquez, 1865):

> *"Entre las innumerables plantas útiles con que la Providencia ha enriquecido el suelo del Imperio Mexicano, ocupa el Maguey un lugar distinguido por las muchas y variadas aplicaciones que de él, y de sus productos se hacen en la medicina, en la veterinaria, y en la economía doméstica; pudiendo suceder fácilmente que cuando se analice y observe con más detención a la luz de la ciencia, se descubran en esta planta nuevas propiedades medicinales en nuevas aplicaciones a la industria.*

> ["Among the innumerable useful plants with which Providence has enriched the estate of the Mexican Empire, Maguey occupies a distinguished place for the multitude of applications derived from it and from its products. These are used in medicine, veterinary science, and the domestic economy; it may very well happen that once this plant is analyzed and observed more carefully in the light of science, novel medical and industrial applications will be found for it."]

The growing interest in mezcal may yet help fulfill the prediction of the Brothers Blasquez. The time has come to hold up the noble maguey to the scrutiny of science. Can the claims be empirically validated? What inspired the brothers to rhapsodize about this desert succulent? Perhaps the claims they made about uses in medicine, for instance, will be further researched and vindicated by contemporary techniques. Galileo Galilei once said, "Measure what is measurable and make measurable what is not so". Studies can be designed to isolate and evaluate the active compounds in agave which may be beneficial to humans and animals.

The name George Washington Carver has become synonymous with the peanut. Someday the Blasquez brothers may occupy a similar place with regard to the agave. Just as Carver faithfully studied the peanut and derived countless useful applications for the previously obscure legume, the Blasquez brothers examined and recorded the attributes of the venerable agave plant and described many of its contemporary applications.

Today, mezcal production generates useful byproducts. Every bottle of mezcal produces 10–12 times its volume in *viñaza*—the acidic solution remaining after distillation—together with 40 pounds (640 ounces or 18 kilograms) of *bagasse*, which is the fibrous residue of the agave plant after it is spent. This means that around 20 million gallons (76 million liters) of viñaza are produced every year (Agave Spectator, 2021).

Producers have learned to upcycle their viñaza and agave fibers to create adobe bricks by marrying the byproducts with earth and sun. Centuries-old adobe construction delights the eye and is an architectural staple in the regions where agave grows.

Other mezcaleros choose to use bagasse as compost to improve the soil in their fields. Many add it to animal feed. Still others upcycle their bagasse into fuel blocks, which they use to heat their stills and reduce their reliance on firewood.

One enterprising producer built a fish farm out of his old fermentation tanks to neutralize the naturally-occuring acid in his viñaza. Charcoal filters and anaerobic bio-digesters filter the viñaza, turning it into clean water. After circulating through a final tank, this purified water is discharged into the local river system. Astonishingly, local authorities tried to stop him from doing this, saying that it would pressure other producers into doing the same. Let us hope that common sense prevails going forward!

As of 2021, the return on investment on agave plantations was as much as 500% (Agave Spectator, 2021). The future for agave and mezcal looks bright. As we have seen, creative producers are able to maintain both artisanal production methods and the cherished way of life of mezcal-producing families. Increasing demand for sustainably-produced mezcals funds innovation, preserves cultural traditions, and implies a vibrant future for these ancient beverages in the decades and even the centuries to come.

BACK TO THE FUTURE

At some point, the current mezcal-making regulations will come up for review. There is talk that when this happens, there will be a new *mixto* category jostling for position in the mezcal universe. If the mixto (or "mixed") category is authorized, mezcal made with less than 100% agave will be approved for sale, broadening the market for agave products (Coss, 2022). Having additional options normally benefits the consumer as well as every individual and entity working to create the merchandise and deliver it to the final buyer. Mezcal-making is ultimately a business and to reach a larger and more distant market a certain amount of industrialization is inevitable, but it is not necessarily undesirable.

Does industrialization doom small producers? At first glance, it appears that they could be squeezed out by a combination of regulatory barriers, competition from large-scale enterprises, and potentially high prices of agave.

However, the consumer might be the savior of small producers. Part of the allure of mezcal is its traditional, family-oriented roots, and many consumers want to sip mezcals that have been produced in this way rather than big-brand spirits. They've heard the stories and sometimes even traveled to Mexico and met the makers of a particular artisanal brand. These relationships appeal to consumers, and they want to be a part of them.

Small brands with a good e-commerce strategy can distribute in one state and expand their network by working with a national retailer based in the United States or another country. Social media provides an excellent platform for them to share their stories with the world. Doing so can rapidly enable the gifted, but obscure descendants of multi-generational mezcalero or farm families to be discovered and to establish strong relationships with those who can help them preserve their traditions while they launch their brands anew. These small but outstanding producers will find their niche in an increasingly global market.

CONCLUSION

In the last few years, mezcal has taken the world by storm.

The noble agave, which has been harvested as a substrate for fermenting alcohol since around 2000 B.C., is more relevant than ever for the cognoscenti of fermented spirits. The carbohydrate-rich heart of the agave takes years to develop, and is highly prized as the exclusive base ingredient for mezcal.

Agaves grow in several parts of the world besides Mexico, where they are often used as a source of fiber and other natural raw materials. Because of their ability to thrive in desert environments, agaves are also a good option for cultivation in the Southwestern United States, which is known for its semi-arid or arid climate.

Grandfather to tequila, mezcal is produced from both wild and cultivated agaves. A wide variety of agave plants are used, although many producers are now turning to espadin, a cultivated variety that is grown as a monocrop specifically for mezcal production, particularly around Oaxaca in southern Mexico. Fueled by increasing demand for agave spirits, wild and unusual agave varieties are sought in the distant countryside. Closer to home, these varieties can be planted on large commercial farms, ejido parcels, or backyard plots.

After collection, the agaves are roasted in giant pits dug into the ground and surrounded by rocks. After a few days, the agaves are removed, broken into smaller pieces, and mashed to a pulp. This is done either by hand, with the help of heavy wooden mallets, or by a tahona, a large circular stone pulled by a donkey or horse. The resulting agave fibers and nectar are collected and amassed in huge vats for natural fermentation using wild yeasts. These yeasts are present in the surrounding environment and feed on the sugar in the agave juices.

Once fermentation ends, the liquid is distilled twice. Sometimes, it is distilled three or even four times! Flavorings are added to the second or later distillate to impart further unique aromas and tastes to the mezcal. In some cases, the resulting spirit is transferred to wooden barrels for aging. Mezcal has been aged for centuries, although some die-hard traditionalists argue that this is not how it was historically produced, at least not by early Spaniards or pioneer Filipinos, and certainly not by ancient Nahualt or Aztec mezcaleros. Nevertheless, aging turns the mezcal amber and imbues a further range of flavors to an already multifaceted spirit. When a drink has been made by diverse people over hundreds of years, it cannot easily be defined by narrow boundaries.

The sudden popularity of a traditional drink that was once produced in backyard stills and reserved for celebrations, festivals, and funerals or even offered to the dead has changed the face of mezcal-producing Mexico. In the mid-1990s, the Mexican government effectively trademarked the name *mezcal*, stipulating that only certain mezcal-producing regions inside Mexico could use it. Producers now need to comply with certification standards, which are sometimes onerous and expensive and may put some traditional production methods at risk. Uncertified producers need to call their output agave spirits. Because of the potential break with tradition, some family-owned producers have elected to remain uncertified.

For mezcal aficionados, the drink pairs delightfully with Oaxacan and other Mexican cuisines, whether used as an ingredient or simply enjoyed to complement the food. Mezcal cocktails have become particularly popular among millennials. This demographic category, most smitten with mezcal in the first place, is driving demand across the world.

As we saw earlier, mezcal has several potential health benefits. Compounds in agave plants and, by extension, mezcal may promote good HDL cholesterol, lower blood pressure, and reduce stress and depression. Because of its antioxidant and anti-inflammatory properties, it may also help keep cancer at bay. Always remember that to derive any health benefits, you must consume mezcal in moderation. A little copita can also be a part of a health-conscious menu because it is low in calories, containing less sugar than other spirits. Enthusiasts have even claimed that because of its purity, mezcal will not give you a hangover if you overindulge. However, I do not recommend the experiment!

The really good news about mezcal is that you can grow your own agaves and produce agave spirits on your own land, the way thousands of Mexican producers have done for generations. We are discussing artisanal spirits, after all! Growing agave plants is not difficult in dry areas or with well-draining soils. Just remember to space them adequately. They do grow to extremely large sizes, and cultivated agave tend to be bigger than wild ones. Having sufficient room for each plant is essential. Once established, the succulents require little water and almost no fertilizer. While you wait for them to mature, you will delight in their dramatic displays of unusual shapes and colors. These garden plants lend themselves well to unusual landscaping. One morning you will notice the impressively tall stem of your first agave flower. It will be a time for photographs and celebration!

We have seen that harvesting agaves can be a tricky operation because of the sheer size of the plants and their piñas, and we have stressed the need for some assistance. We've considered this fantastic opportunity for ending individual isolation and restoring a culture of appreciation. When, after harvest, the chopped pieces of piña are roasted on a homemade fire pit, laughter can sound and stories can begin. Good, satisfying work, being part of a team, making memories together, these are strong building blocks of a community.

When the mezcal is finally ready and your friends gather to sample it, they will appreciate it all the more because of their participation in its creation. They will not be disappointed. Just like snowflakes, each batch of mezcal is unique. The ultimate success and peculiar characteristics of each prized bottle will depend on many variables, from the variety of agave used to the type of still employed for distillation. Modern production techniques have caused consumers to expect an extremely high degree of uniformity in their food and drinks. Mezcal reminds us that life cannot be programmed with certainty, and the unexpected setbacks and joys we experience along the way ought to be the subject of our thoughtful reflection. We only have the illusion of being captains of our destiny, when in fact we are merely ship stewards surveying the mighty ocean and taking in the journey with awe. So it is with mezcal. It makes me glad to know that there are still handcrafted items in our society that cannot consistently be exactly reproduced. Mezcal is a free spirit in a world where regulators seek to standardize and homogenize everything from our food to our clothes, from our education to our healthcare, and from the grass height in our front yards to the suction power of our vacuum cleaners.

Handcrafted products bear the signatures of their human makers. They reflect the chosen values, carefully applied techniques, and even the dreams of the men and women whose livelihood depends on them. This creates their allure. In the case of mezcal, it fosters among young, upwardly mobile professionals a growing interest both in recently discovered or exotic brands, and in the art and science of distillation as a hobby.

Mezcal's unprecedented popularity is creating fresh opportunities for new and existing producers. In the scenic areas where agave spirits are a big part of the economy, new plantings protect the natural environment and ensure economic viability and quality of life for local populations. New plantations, whether on small-scale ejido parcels or larger properties, will help preserve genetic diversity since some neglected varieties, especially rare ancestral strains, can go extinct in the wild. Saving the agave means preserving the heritage of farming families and the local history of entire villages. It means appreciating the inquisitive consumers of mezcal who increase the market value of agave and ensure its long-term demand.

A new economic vitality can spring from this. Today, many rural areas suffer from brain drain as young residents pull up stakes and move to larger cities in search of education and lucrative employment. Their less fortunate neighbors are forced to accept jobs with subsistence wages, often sharing cramped living quarters with others who also have little hope of career advancement. In either case, these emigrants lose their connection with their agrarian heritage and rich cultural history. Without the chance to engage with the land, their traditional practices become nothing more than family stories told to disconnected descendants.

A thriving agave industry fixes this! High demand for mezcal opens the door to many types of jobs. There are entrepreneurial farmers and skilled jimadors who work the land. Palenqueros supervise the production process, and distillery workers facilitate every step from fermentation to bottling.

There are also myriad positions for specialists and skilled professionals. For example, brand ambassadors, social media influencers, and marketing specialists creatively promote demand for mezcal. Chemists and lab technicians closely monitor and adjust the production process to ensure that mezcal is both high-quality and safe for human consumption. There are technical roles in bottling and packaging, and higher paying distribution roles for truck drivers. Export/import specialists help producers to navigate the ever-changing regulatory landscape so that mezcal can be offered in distant lands.

Numerous positions also exist in tourism! Mezcal's popularity brings people from far away. Tour guides may ride burros, bicycles, or buses as they lead enthusiastic groups of thirsty visitors. In some cases, entire families can fill these roles.

Small inns and restaurants serve locally-sourced fare, while wedding and event venues allow the growing numbers of visitors to enjoy spectacular mountain views that had been heretofore overlooked. As people from across Mexico and beyond spend time in these natural settings, they foster an appreciation for the beauty of nature and the values of the small communities that are enjoying a great revival.

Ultimately, the consumer will decide the future of mezcal. The highest demand is currently for homegrown, artisanal drinks. Mezcaleros using traditional production methods can form partnerships with distributors who have larger networks, but there will always be a place for very small producers with top-shelf mezcal and a good story to tell.

If you are able to visit Oaxaca, I encourage you to make the trip. The people are welcoming and the food and beverages are simply unforgettable. I am confident that you will be wowed by the experience of eating a savory dish with the house mole sauce paired with a thoughtfully selected mezcal.

You can also bring a bit of Oaxaca home by making your own mezcal! There is no time like the present to take your first steps into the kaleidoscopic universe of mezcal-making, following in the footsteps of the intrepid mezcaleros who developed their processes one small batch at a time.

This isn't like prepping a microwave dinner. It's an immersive, iterative adventure that blends science and the culinary arts in your personal environment.

My only caution is that once you start experimenting, you may find it hard to stop.

To your health!

¡Salud!

GLOSSARY

ABV: Abbreviation for "Alcohol By Volume"

Agave: Genus or category of plants that are used to make mezcal.

Agavin: A sugar which is naturally found in agave plants, and which cannot be digested and absorbed by the human body. It functions as a prebiotic fiber and may lower blood sugar levels.

Aguardiente: A Spanish term meaning "burning water". The word and the drink are both very old and already existed in medieval times, in various forms, and throughout Europe. The French call theirs "Eau de Vie", or "Water of Life". Historically, there have been many types of aguardiente, all with a high alcohol content and produced from different fruits, vegetables, or plants through fermentation and distillation. Today, individual countries in Europe and the Americas have their own definitions and styles of aguardiente. In a mezcal-related context, aguardiente also describes agave spirits from Guanajuato.

Altiplano: High plains, also known as tableland.

Amate: A handmade paper crafted from tree bark by Mexico's pre-Spanish civilizations.

Añejo: Mezcal class that has been aged in wood for over a year.

Anforita: A small amphora (i.e. a two-handled jar from antiquity), sometimes used as an amulet.

Anti-transpirant: A liquid that is sprayed onto plant foliage to reduce transpiration, which is the exhalation of water vapor through plant stomata.

Apéritif: A French word describing an alcoholic beverage enjoyed before a meal, and which is said to stimulate the appetite.

Autoclave: Stainless steel pressure cooker or steamer that may be used according to denomination of origin (DO) regulations for producing tequila and mezcal.

Bagasse (Bagaso or Bagazo): Agave fibers left over after the mezcal has been produced. They are used to insulate the rocks of the pit oven and to make adobe bricks, as well as for compost, for fires beneath stills, and to seal cracks on clay pots.

Blanco: Also known as joven or white mezcal, this is one of the classifications used for a mezcal that receives no further treatment after distillation is completed.

Blue Weber: Agave variety (*Agave tequilana*) used almost exclusively to make tequila.

Brix: Unit used to determine the dissolved sugar concentration of a liquid.

Bulbil: A small aerial rosette found on the flowering stalk of an agave plant, which can be propagated to produce a clone of the original plant.

Capacha: Referencing alcohol stills developed around 1500 - 1000 B.C. near Colima, Mexico.

Cenizo: The favored agave species (*Agave durangensis*) for mezcal-making in Durango, a state in northwestern Mexico.

Century Plant: A term describing agaves generally but especially slow-growing *Agave americana* because of the many years required for these plants to mature. Although agave usually completes its life cycle in ten to thirty years (rather than a full century), it blooms only once before it senesces.

Chapulín: A roasted grasshopper (*Sphenarium spp.*) that is frequently eaten in parts of Mexico and Central America.

Chef d'oeuvre: The definitive or outstanding work of a creative artisan or craftsman. This is a French term designating the masterpiece with which the maker shapes his or her world.

Chocolate y Café: A chocolate cake infused with coffee.

Coir: A stiff, coarse fiber derived from the outer husks of coconut fruit. The material is often used in doormats, brushes, and mattresses.

Comal: A flat and smooth griddle with shallow edges used for cooking and toasting in Mexico, Central America, and parts of South America.

Común: Liquid that results from the first distillation of agave juice following the end of fermentation.

Convection Freezing: Convection freezing is caused by the physical movement of cold air around warmer surfaces, which results in heat transfer to the air. Lakes are a good example of this phenomenon, as the surface freezes in cold weather due to contact with frigid air while deeper water remains liquid. Convection freezing presents a threat to foliage when cold air blows on plant leaves.

Cooper: A person who crafts or repairs casks and barrels.

Copita: Shallow clay vessel used to serve and/or drink mezcal.

Denomination of origin (DO): Used to define a particular product as exclusive to a certain country. Denomination of origin for mezcal defines mezcal as exclusively Mexican and designates the regions where it can be produced within Mexico.

Digestif: A French term describing an alcoholic beverage enjoyed after a meal, which is said to stimulate digestion.

Diffuser: Equipment used to extract juice from roasted agave.

Dry Fermentation: An optional step in mezcal production which comes after roasting the agave. Only the pulp and juice are fermented, and the mixture is left exposed to the open air to collect microorganisms. If this method is used, it is done before wet fermentation.

Ensemble: Mezcal made from two or more agave varieties, where the mixing takes place during fermentation and distillation.

Ejido: Communal land divided into individual parcels, and used for agriculture by community members. An ejido parcel can only be sold to Mexican citizens, and sales must be approved by the community.

Entrée: The main course of a meal. The word has French origins and literally means "entrance".

Esculent: Something that is edible; suitable for human consumption.

Espadin: A common agave variety that predominates around Oaxaca.

Extra Añejo: Mezcal class that has been aged in wood for over three years.

Fábrica: A palenque in Guerrero.

Filipino still: A simple still wherein evaporation and distillation occur in the same chamber, and which was introduced to Mexico by Filipinos in the 16th century.

Fogonero or Fogonera: An agave roasting specialist in Guerrero.

Fresca: A chilled beverage flavored with sugar, fruit, grains, or seeds.

Galleon: A sailing ship, typically square-rigged with three or more decks and masts. The ship was designed to cross oceans and carry substantial cargo (i.e. cannons for war or merchandise for trade).

Goan: The term describes the people and culture of Goa, India. This is an affluent region on India's west coast.

Hacienda: A landed estate, typically dedicated to farming.

Hierve el Agua: A stunning collection of travertine rock formations that look like waterfalls and are a favorite visitor attraction in San Lorenzo Albarradas, Oaxaca.

Hormesis: A biological phenomenon describing the tendency of living things to adapt to moderate stresses rather than succumb to them. For example, exercise causes short-term disruption to muscle fibers and diminution of cardiac capacity; in the long run, however, it strengthens muscle tissue and promotes heart health. In the same way, exposure to low levels of toxic phytochemicals can stimulate the body to greater resilience and wellness over time.

Insolation: A description of the amount of solar radiation that reaches a surface. More sunshine is equivalent to more insolation.

Jimador: Specialist in agave harvesting.

Jolgorio: Rejoicing, celebrating, and engaging in boisterous fun.

Joven: A young mezcal that has not been aged or was only aged in glass for a short period.

Lambanog: An alcoholic drink originating in the Philippines. It is produced through the fermentation and distillation of coconut sap. Lambanog is a clear to milky white liquor and features an ABV ranging from 40% to 45%.

Madurado en vidrio: This means "matured in glass" in Spanish, and describes mezcal that was stored in glass containers for at least twelve months, whether underground or in a dark indoor cellar with minimal variations in temperature and humidity.

Maguey: Mexican term for agave, especially in Oaxaca.

Matrícula de Tributos: The Spanish term for "Tribute Roll".

Mazo: Large wooden mallet used for crushing roasted agave by hand.

Mercantilist: An adherent of "mercantilism", an economic policy that is designed to maximize exports and minimize imports for a country. By maintaining a positive balance of trade, mercantilism is thought to strengthen national prosperity. The underlying rationale is that a heavily-exporting nation can support a domestic agricultural and manufacturing base, accumulate finite durable assets (i.e. gold bullion), and establish foreign trading monopolies which augment the prices received and support demand for the domestic currency. Mercantilism was the prevalent economic philosophy in the 16th through 18th centuries, and nations generally paid for trade deficits by transferring gold directly to the countries from which they imported goods.

Mesoamerica: An anthropological and geographical term describing the cultural and historic region encompassing central Mexico and northern Central America. The term "meso" comes from Greek and means "middle", so Mesoamerica translates literally as "Middle America".

Mestiza: A woman with mixed racial or ethnic ancestry, especially of European and indigenous descent.

Metl: Nahuatl word for agave.

Mezcal: A distilled alcoholic beverage made from the fermented juice of various types of agave, including but not limited to the Blue Weber agave used in tequila production.

Mezcaleria: A bar which primarily offers mezcal.

Mezcalero or Mezcalera: A person or artisan who makes mezcal.

Mezcla: The Spanish word for "mixture". Describes a combination of different batches of mezcal made at different times and from various agave species.

Minero: Mezcal from Santa Catarina Minas, Ocotlán, Oaxaca.

Mixto: Tequila containing at least 51% Blue Weber agave mixed with fermented agave juice and cane sugar spirits.

Molcajete: In Mexican cuisine, a traditional tool made from volcanic rock. The rough surface is used for grinding food (as with a mortar and pestle). The word comes from the Aztec words for 'seasoning' and 'bowl'.

Montane: Characterized by mountainous and cool-to-cold upland slopes.

Mosto: Fresh agave juice and bagasse (bagazo) derived from cooked, shredded piñas, with water added, and that is ready for fermentation.

Muerto: The Spanish word for "dead", describes agave that has completed fermentation.

Nahuatl: Language of the Aztecs.

Neat: A serving of an alcoholic beverage with no added ice or water. The drink is offered at room temperature.

New Spain: A Spanish colonial territory which existed from 1521-1821 A.D. The official title was the Viceroyalty of New Spain or *Virreinato de Nueva España*. The capital was Mexico City.

Octli Poliuhuquia: The full-length name for "pulque" in Nahualt, the language of the Aztecs.

Ojo de Tigre: This Spanish expression means "Eye of the Tiger".

Ordinario: First distillation of fermented agave mosto.

Oxalate: Salts or esters of oxalic acid, occurring naturally in plants such as agave and rhubarb, oxalates are capable of forming insoluble calcium salts. In healthy people, traces of calcium oxalate are metabolized by the body and present no problem. In individuals with impaired kidney function, these calcium salts can accumulate over time and be impossible to eliminate through the normal route of renal clearance, as they seal the bladder tighter than a Scottish penny jar.

Palenque: Mezcal distillery, often located on the mezcalero's property.

Palenquero or Palenquera: A distillery worker.

Patulin: A naturally-occurring compound classified as a polyketide (i.e. a family of chemicals originating in fungi, bacteria, or plants). It is named after the fungus from which it was isolated, *Penicillium patulum*. Patulin belongs to a class of compounds called "lactones" (i.e. a group of flavoring compounds), and is a heat-stable carcinogen, which means that it can survive baking in a pie placed in an oven.

Pechuga (poultry breast): Traditional style of mezcal preparation where poultry, meat, fruits, herbs, or spices are added to the final distillation to confer extra flavors.

Perlas (pearls): Bubbles that form on the top of mezcal that is between 45% and 55% ABV, and which are often considered a sign of authenticity.

Perlite: A naturally-occuring form of obsidian which has a high water content. The innate hydration causes this type of pale volcanic glass to expand massively when heated. Perlite is used for insulation, or to retain moisture in plant growth media. You can recognize perlite as the small pale granules in potting soil.

Piña: A common Mexican name for the thickened heart of the central agave stem that is used to produce mezcal. It is also the Spanish word for "pineapple".

Pulque: Traditional, mildly alcoholic beverage made by directly fermenting the sap tapped off the agave piña while the plant is still growing.

Pulquería: A tavern specializing in serving pulque.

Pup: An offshoot from the base of a plant, which can be propagated to produce a clone of the original plant.

Quesillo: A semi-hard, low-fat white cheese that is sometimes called Oaxaca cheese.

Quiote: Tall flower stalk that agave plants shoot out when they reach maturity.

Radiation Freezing: The most common form of frost, radiation freezes are caused by the ambient reflection of heat back into space. This is typically associated with a clear night sky, low or no wind, temperature inversion (i.e. cooler temperatures at ground level than in the atmosphere), high aridity and/or low dew point, and air temperatures which fall below freezing at night but remain above freezing during the day.

Reposado: Mezcal that has been aged in wood for 2–12 months.

Sal de Gusano: Worm salt derived from ground moth larvae that usually accompanies mezcal, often with an orange slice.

Saponin: A class of plant glucosides (i.e. chemicals derived from glucose sugar) which is capable of producing a soapy lather. Most of these compounds are toxic, and their presence in foliage may protect plants from grazing animals and insects. Some saponins in edible legumes are actually beneficial to human health, and provide a compelling reason to include beans in one's diet.

Secretaría de Economía: The department in Mexico's federal cabinet responsible for economic matters; in English it is "Secretariat of Economy".

Silvestre: A Spanish term designating plants that grow in the wild.

Smoke: Flavor of mezcal created by the wood-based fire made in earthen pit ovens when the piñas are roasted.

Stomata: The microscopic pores in the epidermis of a plant leaf, which facilitate the movement of gasses in and out of the spaces between plant cells.

Tahona: Traditional, horse-drawn large stone wheel used to crush the roasted piña when making mezcal.

Tajín: A traditional blend of mild spices in Mexican cuisine, consisting principally of dehydrated lime juice, ground red chilies, and sea salt. The seasoning is named after *El Tajín*, an archaeological site in Veracruz, Mexico.

Tannins: A bitter-tasting organic substance found in plant tissues, which consists of derivatives of gallic acid (i.e. a compound found in sumac, gallnuts, tea leaves, oak bark, witch hazel, and other plants). Tannins are naturally present in wine and in many mezcals. When synthetically isolated, tannins are used in leather production and ink manufacturing.

Taproot: A description of the organization of a plant's root system, characterized by a straight central root or taproot which tapers in width as it extends downward vertically. Smaller side rootlets branch off from the taproot. Carrots are a classic example of a plant exhibiting a taproot.

Tepache: Agave juice that has stopped fermenting and is ready for distillation.

Tequila: A distilled alcoholic beverage made from the fermented juice of the Blue Weber agave (*Agave tequilana weber*).

Terpenes: A class of chemical compounds comprised of unsaturated hydrocarbons found in the essential oils of plants, especially citrus and conifers.

Terra Firma: A Latin term describing "dry land", as opposed to the ocean.

Terroir: A French term encompassing a holistic description of the environment in which a particular crop is grown, taking into account factors such as elevation, topography, soil composition, and climate.

Tierra Caliente: Refers to lowlands and means "hot land" in Spanish.

Tina: A round, wooden container that holds liquid.

Topsoil: The top layer of soil on earth, topsoil contains organic matter and beneficial microorganisms, and is the fertile horizon in which plants grow.

Tragedy of the Commons: This expression, coined by American ecologist and microbiologist Garrett Hardin, describes the tendency of individuals to selfishly deplete public or shared resources in the absence of private property. Ownership creates an incentive for conservation as most people take care of what is theirs. However noble the people who set aside land for common enjoyment, their efforts often fail because those who first exploit the land receive all of its benefits at the expense of more responsible users. As an example, two children given a plate of cookies to share will usually hurry to take more than their half, whereas they are more likely to chew slowly and savor their desserts if given their own separate plates. In another context (and in the absence of outside coercion or external inducements), a gardener will tend carefully to her own yard, but will seldom contribute much effort to a random plot of fairway in her local public park.

Tribute Roll: A manuscript compiled by the Aztec Empire to track tax collection from its subjugated peoples. The Spanish term for this is Matrícula de Tributos.

Tuba: An alcoholic drink originating from the Philippines, derived from the sap extracted from diverse palm tree species. The introduction of tuba to Guam, the Mariana Islands, and Mexico occurred during the era of Spanish colonization. It remains popular in Mexico to this day, especially in the states of Colima, Jalisco, Michoacán, Nayarit, and Guerrero.

Vinata: The term used to describe a mezcalero in Durango, Mexico.

Vinatero: The term used to describe a palenque in Durango, Mexico.

Viñaza: Acidic liquid residue of mezcal distillation. It is used for cleaning and to make adobe bricks.

Wet Fermentation: An essential step in mezcal production which comes after roasting the agave. Water is added to the crushed agave fibers, and the mosto is left in vats to ferment. Wet fermentation is often the only kind of fermentation that takes place, but is only implemented after dry fermentation if both wet and dry methods are used.

Xeriscape: A style of landscape design requiring minimal or no irrigation. This is a popular method in arid regions, and has the added benefit of needing very little maintenance (i.e. mowing or Fall leaf collection).

Zakuski: Bite-sized hors d'oeuvres served cold and typically consumed between sips of vodka or another alcoholic drink.

REFERENCES

48 hours in Oaxaca—a mezcal tasting. (2012, August 22). Gastronomista. https://www.gastronomista.com/2012/08/42-hours-in-oaxaca-mezcal-tasting.html

Admin. (2019, August 19). *Gastronomy of Oaxaca—Tourist guide.* Visit Mexico. https://www.visit-mexico.mx/oaxaca/gastronomy-of-oaxaca

Agave. (n.d.). Gardenia. https://www.gardenia.net/genus/agaves

Agave americana var. oaxacensis. (n.d.). Mezcalistas. https://www.mezcalistas.com/agave_species/agave-americana-var-oaxacensis/#:

Agave growth and harvest. (2023, January 24). Academia Patrón. https://www.academiapatron.com/study-guide/agave-growth-and-harvest#:

Agave growth and harvesting. (2022, July 26). Academia Patrón. https://www.academiapatron.com/making-tequila/agave-growth-and-harvesting/anatomy-reproduction

Agave harvesting—How to harvest agave nectar. (n.d.). Mezcal Rosaluna: Mezcal Is Magic. https://mezcalrosaluna.com/article/agave-harvesting

Agave Spectator. (2021a, April 22). *Part one: Cooperation versus domination and mezcal sustainability.* https://agavespectator.com/agave-shorts/f/part-one-cooperation-versus-domination-and-mezcal-sustainability

Agave Spectator. (2021b, April 26). *Part two: Cooperation versus domination and mezcal sustainability.* https://agavespectator.com/agave-shorts/f/part-two-cooperation-versus-domination-and-mezcal-sustainability

Akim, T. (2020, September 3). *Why this spirit is considered the healthiest alcohol.* Forbes. https://www.forbes.com/sites/tanyaakim/2020/09/03/the-healthiest-alcohol/?sh=47dc90101475

Alcohol Free Wellness. (2022, February 16). *Is wine Paleo? Surely.* https://www.drinksurely.com/a/blog/is-wine-paleo#table-of-contents-2

Alex. (2023, August 4). *How mezcal is made—the 6+1 steps of mezcal production.* Mezcal Pro. https://mezcalpro.com/blog/how-mezcal-is-made-the-ultimate-guide

Allen, M. (2023, August 7). *Mezcal BBQ sauce recipe.* Mezcal El Salencio. https://www.silencio.com/newsletter-3/mezcal-barbecue-sauce-recipe

Andrews, B. (2023, August 15). *The 12 best reposado tequilas to drink in 2024.* Liquor.com. https://www.liquor.com/best-reposado-tequilas-5088494

Arellano-Plaza, M., et al. (2022). *Mezcal production in Mexico: Between tradition and commercial exploitation.* Frontiers in Sustainable Food Systems, 6. https://doi.org/10.3389/fsufs.2022.832532

AZ Quotes. (n.d.). *Louis L'Amour Quote*. https://www.azquotes.com/quote/1147284

Baird, S. (2016, June 23). *Meet mezcal's traditional sidekicks*. Punch. https://punch drink.com/articles/traditional-mezcal-food-pairings-and-bar-snacks/

Banda Yurirense (2023). *El Desierto*. Iván Gonzalez. Plata o cobre. Translation by author. https://www.musixmatch.com/es/letras/Banda-Yurirense/El-Desierto

Bank, L., & Periban, C. (2020). *How many agaves does it take to make a bottle of mezcal?* Agave Road Trip. https://agaveroadtrip.com/episodes/s2e22-how-many-agaves-does-it-take-to-make-a-bottle-of-mezcal

Barbezat, S. (2019, May 7). *How Oaxacan mezcal plays a vital role in the local culture*. Discover by Silversea. https://discover.silversea.com/travel-tips/food-drink/oaxacan-mezcal-in-local-culture

Bard Ugo, L. (n.d.). *A quote from The Language of Thorns*. Goodreads. https://www.goodreads.com/quotes/9074933-love-speaks-in-flowers-truth-requires-thorns

Bayless, R. (n.d.). *Oaxaca with Rick Bayless*. Viking Range. https://www.vikingrange.com/consumer/product/more-viking/the-viking-life/food-and-wine-articles/oaxaca-with-rick-bayless#:

Ben & Anthony. (n.d.). *Mezcal production by region*. Mezcal Mal Bien. https://www.mezcalmalbien.com/by-region

BevAlc Insights Team. (2022, June 29). *Category on the rise: Mezcal*. BevAlc Insights. https://bevalcinsights.com/category-on-the-rise-mezcal

Blasquez, Pedro and Blasquez, Ignacio (1865). *Memoria Sobre el Maguey Mexicano (Agave Maximilianea)*. https://www.google.com/books/edition/Memoria_sobre_el_Maguey_Mexicano/t6FXAAAAcAAJ

Bourdain, A. (2018, January 10). *Bourdain, off the cuff: Mexico*. Explore Parts Unknown. https://explorepartsunknown.com/mexico/bourdain-off-the-cuff-mexico

Brainy Quote. (n.d.). *Joyce Carol Oates quotes*. https://www.brainyquote.com/quotes/joyce_carol_oates_100218

Brostad, M. (2023, April 25). *Harvesting agave: A step-by-step guide to a sustainable process*. Shuncy. https://shuncy.com/article/how-should-agave-be-harvested

Brown, J. (2022, September 29). *Just don't call it tequila: The global agave boom has arrived*. Wine Enthusiast. https://www.wineenthusiast.com/culture/spirits/agave-around-the-world

Bryan, L. (2023, May 3). *The best ceviche recipe*. Downshiftology. https://downshiftology.com/recipes/ceviche/#wprm-recipe-container-66752

Bryan, L. and Singh, A. (2024, May 7). *Alcohol and Sleep*. Sleep Foundation. https://www.sleepfoundation.org/nutrition/alcohol-and-sleep

Butler, N. (2017, September 20). *Salmon: Health benefits, facts, and research*. Www.medicalnewstoday.com. https://www.medicalnewstoday.com/articles/307811

California Department of Fish and Wildlife. (n.d.). *California laws protecting native plants*. https://wildlife.ca.gov/Conservation/Plants/Laws

Carnot, S. (n.d.). *A quote from Reflections on the Motive Power of Fire*. Goodreads. https://www.goodreads.com/quotes/11785731-the-production-of-heat-alone-is-not-sufficient-to-give

Carreno, G. (n.d.). *Nuestra Historia*. Real Minero. https://realminero.com.mx/our-story

Casa Silencio. (n.d.). *Premium mezcals*. Mezcal el Silencio. https://www.silencio.com/spirits

Cawood, C. (2023a, May 15). *Is the industrialization of mezcal inevitable?* The Spirits Business. https://www.thespiritsbusiness.com/2023/05/is-the-industrialisation-of-mezcal-inevitable/

Cawood, C. (2023b, November 22). *Alternative agave spirits on the rise*. The Spirits Business. https://www.thespiritsbusiness.com/2023/11/alternative-agave-spirits-on-the-rise/#:

Chadwick, I. (2007, June 27). *Cultivating tequila*. In Search of the Blue Agave. https://www.ianchadwick.com/tequila/harvesting.htm#top

Chatham Imports. (2023, August 21). *Los siete misterios*. Chatham Imports Inc. https://www.chathamimports.com/brands/los-siete-misterios

Cheung, E. M. (2021, November 25). *The history of Mexico's agave spirits*. Latina. https://latina.com/the-history-of-mexicos-agave-spirits

Chilled Magazine. (2019, May 1). *Mixing with mezcal*. Chilled. https://issuu.com/chilledmagazine/docs/chilled_v12-i2_issuu/s/104934

Claire. (2012, April 20). *Habanero infused mezcal*. Sel et Sucre. https://www.seletsucre.com/habanero-infused-mezcal

Clarke, P. (2018, April 30). *The Oaxaca old fashioned recipe*. Serious Eats. https://www.seriouseats.com/the-oaxaca-old-fashioned-cocktail-tequila-mezcal-recipe

Cobbs, K. (2022, May 9). *Cooking from the bar cart: Mezcal meets melted cheese*. Garden & Gun. https://gardenandgun.com/recipe/cooking-from-the-bar-cart-mezcal-meets-melted-cheese

Cocina, L. (2013, November 1). *Mole negro, Oaxaca style*. Lola's Cocina. https://lolascocina.com/mole-negro-with-chicken

Cortes, R. R. (2021, December 27). *Agave: Producing an excellent crop (part 2)*. Casa Sauza. https://www.casasauza.com/en/tequila-process/agave-producing-an-excellent-crop-part-2

Cory, H., Passarelli, S., Szeto, J., Tamez, M., Mattei. J. (2018, September 21) *The Role of Polyphenols in Human Health and Food Systems: A Mini-Review*. Frontiers in Nutrition.https://www.ncbi.nlm.nih.gov/pmc/articles/PMC6160559/

Coss, S. (2019a, April 2). *Durango is not Oaxaca, and that is just fine*. Mezcalistas. https://www.mezcalistas.com/durango-is-not-oaxaca-and-that-is-just-fine

Coss, S. (2019b, July 10). *On the mezcal road in San Luis Potosi—Part 1*. Mezcalistas. https://www.mezcalistas.com/on-the-mezcal-road-in-san-luis-potosi-2

Coss, S. (2022, December 29). *Mezcal is mainstream, so now what?* Mezcalistas. https://www.mezcalistas.com/mezcal-is-mainstream-so-now-what

Crosby, B. (1934). Cole Porter and Robert Fletcher. https://lyrics.lyricfind.com/en-GB/lyrics/great-vocalists-dont-fence-me-in

Danao, K. (2021, November 7). *100 cactus quotes to help you endure amidst adversities*. Quote Ambition. https://www.quoteambition.com/cactus-quotes/#google_vignette

de Gramont, B. M. (2022, February 4). *Tequila must be made from a secific type of agave plant—here's why it matters*. Business Insider. https://www.businessinsider.com/guides/kitchen/what-is-tequila-made-from

DeFilippo, C. (2023, January 17). *Roasted pineapple mezcal*. W&P. https://wandp.com/blogs/fresh-squeeze/69701571-roasted-pineapple-mezcal

Didonato, J. (2022, November 1). *15 of the healthiest alcoholic drinks, straight from dietitians*. Byrdie. https://www.byrdie.com/healthiest-alcoholic-drinks-5183917

Doochin, B. (2015, May 16). *How to make mezcal like your grandfather*. Nowhere Men TV. https://nowheremen.tv/2015/05/16/how-to-make-mezcal-like-your-grandfather/

Doran, K. (2023, September 20). *How to make tequila: A distiller's guide*. Mile Hi Distilling. https://milehidistilling.com/how-to-make-tequila/

Downs, L. (2011). *Mezcalito*. Pecados y Milagros. Written by Lila Downs and Paul Cohen. Translation by author. https://www.last.fm/music/Lila+Downs/_/Mezcalito/+lyrics

Douglas, M. (2023, July 25). *160 Mexico quotes & Mexico Instagram captions to inspire you*. Mexico Travel Secrets. https://www.mexicotravelsecrets.com/mexico-quotes-and-mexico-captions/

Drummond, R. (2020, November 24). *Grilled pineapple with cream*. Food Network. https://www.foodnetwork.com/recipes/ree-drummond/grilled-pineapple-with-cream-8853985

Eastman, R. (n.d.). *Every bottle of mezcal tells a story*. San Francisco Tequila Shop. https://sftequilashop.com/pages/every-bottle-of-mezcal-tells-a-story#:

Eby, M. (2023, January 10). *What's the difference between tequila and mezcal?* Food & Wine. https://www.foodandwine.com/cocktails-spirits/differences-between-tequila-mezcal

El Bandolero Meño Sanchez (2023). *El Amo Del Desierto*. La Vida Del Rancho. Translation by author. https://www.boomplay.com/lyrics/145871406

Ellenwood, J. (2023, May 5). *Waiter, why Is there a worm in my tequila?* The Crafty Cask. https://thecraftycask.com/craft-spirits-liqueurs/worm-in-tequila/#:

Emen, J. (2019, December 1). *The emerging world of American agave spirits.* Distiller. https://distiller.com/articles/the-emerging-world-of-american-agave-spirits

Emen, J. (2022, April 4). *Overcoming the risks of mezcal's huge growth.* SevenFifty Daily. https://daily.sevenfifty.com/overcoming-the-risks-of-mezcals-huge-growth/

Emma. (2020, May 5). *Refined sugar-free mezcal margarita.* Emma Eats & Explores. https://emmaeatsandexplores.com/mezcal-margarita/

English, C. (2012, September 12). *A few things learned in the agave fields in Mexico.* Alcademics. https://www.alcademics.com/2012/09/a-few-things-learned-in-the-agave-fields-in-mexico.html

Falkowitz, M. (2023, May 25). *A guide to mezcal: How it's made and which bottles to try.* Serious Eats. https://www.seriouseats.com/guide-to-mezcal

Food Network Kitchen. (2022, June 10). *What is tequila made from?* Food Network. https://www.foodnetwork.com/how-to/packages/food-network-essentials/what-is-tequila-made-from

Fosley. (2023, September). *Mezcal infusions.* Reddit. https://www.reddit.com/r/Mixology/comments/15w1dx3/mezcal_infusions

Fouada, A., Yamina, S., Nait, M.A., Mohammed, B., Abdlekrim, R. (2006). *In Vitro and in Vivo Antilithiasic Effect of Saponin Rich Fraction Isolated From Herniaria hirsuta.* Brazilian Journal of Nephrology. https://bjnephrology.org/wp-content/uploads/2019/11/jbn_v28n4a04.pdf

Francis, M. (2015, January 3). *Edible agave americana. Wild Food Foraging.* The Homestead Survival. https://thehomesteadsurvival.com/edible-agave-americana-wild-food-foraging/

Francisco, M., et al. (2012, October). Ingeniero bioquímico que presenta: *"Desarrollo de los protocolos para la preparación del fermentador semilla, en el proceso de fermentación para la elaboración de mezcal."* Instituto Tecnológico de Tuxtla Gutiérrez. http://repositoriodigital.tuxtla.tecnm.mx/xmlui/bitstream/handle/123456789/891/48609.pdf?sequence=1&isAllowed=y

Franklin, D. (2023, August 11). *A history of mezcal: Tracing mezcal's roots through time.* Drinks Geek. https://drinksgeek.com/history-of-mezcal

Garrone, M. (2017, March 21). *Mixing your mezcals.* Mezcalistas. https://www.mezcalistas.com/mixing-your-mezcals

Genus Agave. (n.d.). The Desert Museum. https://www.desertmuseum.org/books/nhsd_agave.php

George Santayana Quote: "The Best Men in All Ages Keep Classic Traditions Alive." Inspirational Quotes on Beautiful Wallpapers - QuoteFancy. Accessed June 6,

2024. https://quotefancy.com/quote/996164/George-Santayana-The-best-men-in-all-ages-keep-classic-traditions-alive

Gerrone, M. (2020, November 28). *What you need to know about Mexico's hottest mezcal region.* Liquor.com. https://www.liquor.com/articles/san-luis-potosi-mezcal

Glueck, R. (2019, May 8). *A visit with Guerrero's mezcaleros.* El Refugio. https://www.elrefugiobaja.com/blog-main/2019/5/8/a-diamond-in-the-rough

Gluek, R. (2019, March 11). *Mezcal: The making of a masterpiece.* El Refugio. https://www.elrefugiobaja.com/blog-main/2019/3/11/mezcal-the-making-of-a-masterpiece#:

Goldberg, E. (2015, July 4). *We're in Love With Bacanora, the Missing Link Between Tequila and Mezcal.* Bon Appétit. https://www.bonappetit.com/drinks/article/bacanora-mezcal-tequila

Gómez-Ruiz, E. P., & Lacher, T. E. (2019). *Climate change, range shifts, and the disruption of a pollinator-plant complex.* Scientific Reports, 9(1), 14048. https://doi.org/10.1038/s41598-019-50059-6

Gonzalez, D. (2022, February 22). *What is mezcal, what does it taste like and how is it made?* AZ Central. https://www.azcentral.com/in-depth/news/local/arizona/2022/02/22/mezcal-tequila-difference-taste-how-made/6668433001/

Graham, C. (2022, December 15). *Do you know the history and different styles of tequila?* The Spruce Eats. https://www.thespruceeats.com/all-about-tequila-760706

Gritzer, D. (2019, May 28). *El derby ahumado (basil julep with cucumber, jalapeño, and mezcal) Recipe.* Serious Eats. https://www.seriouseats.com/smoked-derby-julep-cucumber-jalapeno-mezcal-recipe

Guanajuato Blog. (2021, November 11). *Experience the home of mezcal in Guanajuato.* Travel Pulse. https://www.travelpulse.com/voices/blogs/experience-the-home-of-mezcal-in-guanajuato

Gunnars, K., & Kelly, E. (2023, November 16). *The Paleo diet—a beginner's guide & meal plan.* Healthline. https://www.healthline.com/nutrition/paleo-diet-meal-plan-and-menu#foods-to-eat

Hank. (2019, April 9). *The evolution of Vida—Part 1.* Del Maguey Single Village Mezcal. https://delmaguey.com/the-evolution-of-vida-3-3

Hatchett, C. (2023, April 27). *How a centuries-old Filipino distilling method helped shape modern Mexican mezcal distilling.* Liquor.com. https://www.liquor.com/filipino-mexico-mezcal-distilling-7485906

Hawk, S. E. M. (2022, November 7). *Is wine Paleo friendly?* Dry Farm Wines. https://www.dryfarmwines.com/blogs/a-matter-of-taste/is-wine-paleo-friendly

History—Del Maguey Single Village mezcal (NOM-041X). (n.d.). Difford's Guide. https://www.diffordsguide.com/producers/1451/del-maguey-single-village-mezcal#:

Holland, M. (2023, April 18). *How to grow and care for an agave plant*. BBC Gardeners World Magazine. https://www.gardenersworld.com/how-to/grow-plants/agave-plant/

Hosea 13:5-God's anger. (n.d.). Bible Hub. https://biblehub.com/hosea/13-5.htm

M. R. F. (2021, February). *Mezcal market to demonstrate a strong growth over 2026*. https://www.marketresearchfuture.com/blogs/mezcal-its-significance-and-the-impact-on

Irish coffee. (n.d.). Nutritionix. https://www.nutritionix.com/food/irish-coffee

Isabel. (2020, December 7). *Queso fundido*. Isabel Eats. https://www.isabeleats.com/queso-fundido

Ivan. (2020, February 4). *The history, rumors, and myths of mezcal*. Madre Restaurants. https://madrerestaurants.com/the-history-rumors-and-myths-of-mezcal

Janzen, E. (2022, February 15). *The ongoing fight over who owns "mezcal"*. Eater. https://www.eater.com/22929882/mezcal-destilado-de-agave-distilling-indigenous-culture-oaxaca

Kachroo-Levine, M. (2021, September 17). *This brand-new Oaxaca hotel is a working mezcal distillery with six perfectly designed suites*. Travel + Leisure. https://www.travelandleisure.com/hotels-resorts/mezcal-casa-silencio-hotel-xaaga-mexico

Kirby, S. (2023, April 27). *99 of the best cactus quotes and sayings*. Everyday Power. https://everydaypower.com/cactus-quotes-and-sayings

Koschel, S. (2016, October 14). *Big things have small beginnings*. https://www.linkedin.com/pulse/big-things-have-small-beginnings-sandra-koschel

Kresser, C. (2019, August 30). *Paleo and wine: Should you drink?* Chris Kresser. https://chriskresser.com/paleo-and-wine-should-you-drink

Kristen. (2019, June 11). *Instant pot smoky mezcal pulled pork tacos*. Feast in Thyme. https://feastinthyme.com/instant-pot-smoky-mezcal-pulled-pork-tacos

La Luna Mezcal. (2021a, July 27). *Mezcal glossary | Mezcal terminology and common expressions*. https://www.lalunamezcal.com/usa/glossary

La Luna Mezcal. (2021b, December 30). *Mezcal regions in Mexico*. https://www.lalunamezcal.com/usa/mezcal-regions-in-mexico

La Luna Mezcal. (2022a, May 10). *7 keys to recognizing a good mezcal*. https://www.lalunamezcal.com/usa/keys-to-recognizing-a-good-mezcal/

La Luna Mezcal. (2022b, September 6). *We tell you 8 benefits of mezcal*. https://www.lalunamezcal.com/usa/we-tell-you-8-benefits-of-mezcal

Lalo. (2018, March 23). *Philosophy*. Mezcal Lalocura. https://www.mezcallalocura.com/philosophy

Lampert, T. R. (n.d.). *Durango*. Mezcal reviews. https://www.mezcalreviews.com/filter-by/state/durango

Lampert, T. R. (2019, August 19). *Michoacan: 400 years of mezcal history*. Mezcalistas. https://www.mezcalistas.com/michoacan-400-years-of-mezcal-history

Lampert, T. R. (2022a, July 5). *Agaves of Puebla*. Mezcalistas. https://www.mezcalistas.com/agaves-of-puebla/

Lampert, T. R. (2022b, September 13). *10 things to know about mezcal poblano*. Mezcalistas. https://www.mezcalistas.com/10-things-to-know-about-mezcal-poblano

Lampert, T. R. (2023, December 26). *What to pair with mezcal*. Mezcalistas. https://www.mezcalistas.com/what-to-pair-with-mezcal

Lange, L. (2023, December 28). *Shrimp mezcal*. Recipe Girl. https://www.recipegirl.com/shrimp-mezcal

Larum, D. (2022, October 8). *Different agave plants—commonly grown agaves In gardens*. Gardening KnowHow. https://www.gardeningknowhow.com/ornamental/cacti-succulents/agave/common-agave-plant-varieties.htm

Leite, D. (2020, January 19). *Lamb barbacoa*. Leite's Culinaria. https://leitesculinaria.com/272689/recipes-lamb-barbacoa.html#wprm-recipe-container-380200

Lensink, M. (2018, April 26). *Mexican chocolate cake with cinnamon frosting*. Nourish and Fete. https://www.nourish-and-fete.com/mexican-chocolate-cake

Lewis, K. (n.d.). *Mezcal process*. Alipus USA. https://alipususa.com/mezcal-process/distillation

Liew, A. (2022, August 24). *Keto margarita | Zero carbs and sugar!* The Big Man's World. https://thebigmansworld.com/keto-margarita/#wprm-recipe-container-51774

Liquor.com. (2023, April 22). *The mezcal mule isn't just another Moscow mule variation*. Liquor.com. https://www.liquor.com/recipes/mezcal-mule

Lopez-Alt, J. K. (2019, May 10). *Spicy hot chocolate with chili, cinnamon, and mezcal recipe*. Serious Eats. https://www.seriouseats.com/spicy-aztec-hot-chocolate-with-chili-cinnamon-mezcal-recipe

Lynch, L. (2019a, May 4). *Smoky basil Oaxacan mezcal cocktail*. A Food Lover's Kitchen. https://afoodloverskitchen.com/oaxacan-mezcal-cocktail/#recipe

Lynch, L. (2019b, August 4). *Peach mezcal margarita recipe*. A Food Lover's Kitchen. https://afoodloverskitchen.com/peach-mezcal-margarita/#recipe

Mafit, D. (2017, November 15). *25 terms every tequila and mezcal drinker should know*. Thrillist. https://www.thrillist.com/spirits/tequila/tequila-and-mezcal-terminology

Maguey tepeztate. (n.d.). Grulani. https://grulani.com/en/agaves/maguey-tepeztate-2/

Markoski, M., et al. (2020). *Molecular Properties of Red Wine Compounds and Cardiometabolic Benefits*. Nutrition and Metabolic Insights. https://www.ncbi.nlm.nih.gov/pmc/articles/PMC4973766/

Martínez-Gallegos, V., et al. (2018). *First report of phosphate-solubilizing bacteria associated with agave angustifolia*. International Journal of Agricultural Biology, 20(6).

https://doi.org/10.17957/IJAB/15.0630

Marx, S. (2023, November 15). *Oysters Oaxacafeller recipe*. Serious Eats. https://www.seriouseats.com/oysters-oaxacafeller

Mayo Clinic Staff. (2020, August 25). *Paleo diet: What is it and why is it so popular?* Mayo Foundation for Medical Education and Research. https://www.mayoclinic.org/healthy-lifestyle/nutrition-and-healthy-eating/in-depth/paleo-diet/art-20111182

McEvoy, J. P. (2013, March 1). *How many varieties of agave can be used to make mezcal? (Take 2)*. Mezcal PhD. https://mezcalphd.com/2013/03/how-many-varieties-of-agave-can-be-used-to-make-mezcal-take-2/

McKirdy, T. (2020, April 15). *All the different types of mezcal, explained*. VinePair. https://vinepair.com/articles/different-types-mezcal-explained/

Meghan. (2022, June 3). *Spicy infused mezcal*. Cake 'N Knife. https://www.cakenknife.com/spicy-infused-mezcal/#:

Meneses, F. (2021, September 10). *Presentan la ruta del mezcal en Puebla*. México Ruta Mágica. https://mexicorutamagica.mx/2021/09/10/presentan-ruta-del-mezcal-en-puebla

Mexico Ideas. (2020, August 29). *Mezcal, the holy elixir*. Mexico Ideas, History & Culture. https://mexicoideas.com/mezcal-mexico

Mezcal Basics. (2019, September 14). Experience agave. https://www.experienceagave.com/mezcal-basics

Mezcal Reviews-The best place to discover and review mezcals. (n.d.). Mezcal Reviews. https://www.mezcalreviews.com

Mezcal Siente Misterios. (n.d.). *Mezcal Los Siete Misterios—El mejor mezcal del mundo mundial!* https://www.sietemisterios.com

Mezcal Tip No. 1: "Sip it. Don't shoot it". (2014, March 29). Los Angeles Times. https://www.latimes.com/food/la-xpm-2014-mar-29-la-fo-virbila-sidebar3-20140329-story.html

Mezcal Vago. (2012). *The history of Mezcal Vago*. https://mezcalvago.com/about

Mezcaleria (n.d.) *Protected Designations of Origin for mezcal and tequila*. Mezcaleria Berlin. https://www.mezcaleria.de/en/mezcal-tequila-protected-origin

Mezcouting. Mezcouting. Accessed June 6, 2024. https://www.mezcouting.com/about-us

Miller, K. (n.d.). *A quote from The Book of Flying*. Goodreads. https://www.goodreads.com/quotes/258355-a-forest-is-mystery-but-the-desert-is-truth-life

Montero, A. (2024, January 1). *¿Cuántos Grados de Alcohol Contiene el Mezcal?* Bares Rentables. https://baresrentables.com/cuantos-grados-de-alcohol-tiene-el-mezcal

Moody Blooms. (2021, September 2). *Agave plant types | Best agave varieties*. Moodybloomsco.com. https://moodybloomsco.com/agave-plant-types-best-agave-varieties/#google_vignette

Mordor Intelligence. (2023). *Mezcal market trends.* Www.mordorintelligence.com. https://www.mordorintelligence.com/industry-reports/mezcal-market/market-trends

Moreno, S. (2021, March 4). *Mezcal agave varieties to try beyond espadín.* Distiller. https://distiller.com/articles/mezcal-agave-varieties

Morgan, A. (2023, April 25). *When it comes to agave spirits, tequila and mezcal are just the beginning.* Liquor.com. https://www.liquor.com/a-guide-to-other-agave-spirits-5271518

Nabhan, G. P. (n.d.). *Salmon with bacanora.* Mezcal Mankind Mutualism. https://www.mezcalmankindmutualism.com/venue/blackened-salmon-with-bacanora

National Geographic Society. (2022, July 16). *Photosynthesis.* National Geographic. https://education.nationalgeographic.org/resource/photosynthesis

Newman, K. (2023, April 26). *How should you select and sip mezcal? Agave experts share their tips.* Liquor.com. https://www.liquor.com/articles/how-to-drink-mezcal-right

Nirumand, M.C., Hajialyani, M., Rahimi, R., Farzaei, M.H., Zingue, S., Nabavi, S.M., and Bishayee, A. (2018, March 7). *Dietary Plants for the Prevention and Management of Kidney Stones: Preclinical and Clinical Evidence and Molecular Mechanisms.* International Journal of Molecular Sciences. https://www.ncbi.nlm.nih.gov/pmc/articles/PMC5877626/

Marina, UEM. (2017, February 23). *NORMA Oficial Mexicana NOM-070-SCFI-2016, Bebidas alcohólicas-Mezcal-Especificaciones.* Diario Oficial de la Federación. https://dof.gob.mx/nota_detalle.php?codigo=5472787&fecha=23/02/2017#gsc.tab=0

November 10, L. B., & Am, 2022 6:46. (2022, November 10). *Barrel-aged mezcal is a uniquely delicious spirit.* Inside Hook. https://www.insidehook.com/drinks/barrel-aged-mezcal

Oaxaca and mezcal, a never-ending story. (n.d.). Mezcal Devoción. https://mezcaldevocion.com/en/2023/02/04/oaxaca-and-mezcal-a-never-ending-story/

Oaxacan Drunken Salsa (salsa borracha de Oaxaca). (2021, July 6). My Hungry Traveler. https://myhungrytraveler.com/cuisines/mexican/oaxacan-drunken-salsa/

Orozco, B. J. (2023, April 27). *What is pulque? A guide to Mexico's ancestral beverage.* Liquor.com. https://www.liquor.com/pulque-drink-explainer-7485913#:

Osigwe, C. (2023, November). *Mezcal's dilemma: Tradition, globalization, and the battle for authenticity.* History. https://vocal.media/history/mezcal-s-dilemma-tradition-globalization-and-the-battle-for-authenticity

Pardilla, C. (2015, March 4). *Beyond tequila: Alternative agave spirits to know.* Eater. https://www.eater.com/2015/3/4/8126129/beyond-tequila-alternative-agave-spirits-to-know

Payne, M. (2017, May 23). *Mezcal and the magic of Oaxaca, Mexico.* The Manual. https://www.themanual.com/travel/visit-oaxaca-city-mexico

Petruzzello, M. (2023, December 29). *Sisal | plant species.* Encyclopedia Britannica. https://www.britannica.com/plant/sisal

Pinson, J. (2023, March 8). *Scientists uncover the unexpected identity of mezcal worms.* Florida Museum. https://www.floridamuseum.ufl.edu/science/scientists-uncover-the-unexpected-identity-of-mezcal-worms/#:

Pringle, W. B. (n.d.). *A quote by Wyatt B Pringle, Jr.* Good Reads. https://www.goodreads.com/quotes/11827902-when-the-heat-is-on-make-sure-you-re-not-that

Producer Profile: Rey Campero Mezcal. (2018, January 16). Ultimate Beverage Challenge. https://www.ultimate-beverage.com/blog/producer-profile-rey-campero-mezcal

Pulled pork tacos. (n.d.). Nutronix. https://www.nutritionix.com/food/pulled-pork-tacos

Quotes Pedia. (n.d.). *If you want to go fast go alone. If you want to go far go together. - African Proverb.* https://www.quotespedia.org/authors/a/african-proverbs/if-you-want-to-go-fast-go-alone-if-you-want-to-go-far-go-together-african-proverb/

Resendiz, C. (2023, October 25). *Las barricas para añejar el tequila y el mezcal.* Destilando México. https://destilandomexico.mx/sobre-el-tequila/las-barricas-para-anejar-el-tequila-y-el-mezcal

Rockne, K. (2019). BrainyQuote. https://www.brainyquote.com/quotes/knute_rockne_103969

Rojo, M. (2023, February 10). *Amid global mezcal craze, scientists and communities try out sustainable plantations.* Mongabay. https://news.mongabay.com/2023/02/amid-global-mezcal-craze-scientists-and-communities-try-out-sustainable-plantations/

Rooney, B. (2023, February 18). *Siete misterios doba yej mezcal: The ultimate bottle guide.* Tasting Table. https://www.tastingtable.com/1199008/siete-misterios-doba-yej-mezcal-the-ultimate-bottle-guide

Rubenstein, G. (2015, September 15). *Mezcal's dance with extinction.* Craftsmanship Magazine. https://craftsmanship.net/mezcals-dance-with-extinction

Ryan. (2023, November 7). *The art of sipping.* The Lost Explorer Mezcal. https://thelostexplorermezcal.com/journal/the-art-of-sipping

Sante, C. de. (2023, October 5). *Is tequila Paleo?* Casa de Sante. https://casadesante.com/blogs/gut-health/is-tequila-paleo

Scarlet. (2020, September 29). *The coolest quarantine project ever? Making an agave spirit at home.* Taste Tequila. https://tastetequila.com/2020/the-coolest-quaran

tine-project-ever/

Score, B. (2018, April 18). *Jalapeno mezcal margarita—spicy and smoky!* A Farmgirl's Dabbles. https://www.afarmgirlsdabbles.com/jalapeno-mezcal-margarita-recipe/#mv-creation-83-jtr

Score, B. (2022, April 8). *Prosecco margarita: how to make a pitcher of margarita!* A Farmgirl's Dabbles. https://www.afarmgirlsdabbles.com/prosecco-margaritas-big-batch-cocktail-recipe/#mv-creation-62-jtr

Shelley. (2022, June 29). *Best mezcal from Oaxaca: 25 must-try brands in 2024.* Travel to Oaxaca. https://traveltooaxaca.com/best-mezcal-from-oaxaca-mexico

Smiths Agency (n.d.). *Holiday grapefruit chiffon cake.* Eggland's Best. https://www.egglandsbest.com/recipe/holiday-grapefruit-chiffon-cake

Southwest, T. A. (n.d.). *Agave species of west and southwest USA.* The American Southwest. https://www.americansouthwest.net/plants/agavoideae/agave.html

Spicer, K. (2023, April 16). *How to grow and care for agave.* Gardener's Path. https://gardenerspath.com/plants/succulents/grow-agave

Starkman, A. (2018, September 26). *Mexico (Oaxaca) mezcal boom dramatically impacts revenue.* Oaxaca, Mezcal & Pulque. https://www.oaxaca-mezcal.com/alvins-blog/mexico-oaxaca-mezcal-boom-dramatically-impacts-revenue

Starkman, A. (2021, June 24). *Is your mezcal a mezcla, an ensamble, or a blend?* Oaxaca, Mezcal % Pulque. https://www.oaxaca-mezcal.com/alvins-blog/is-your-mezcal-a-mezcla-an-ensamble-or-a-blend

Stephens, H. (2023, January 9). *Move over, mezcal. A sustainable tequila alternative Is taking over.* Modern Farmer. https://modernfarmer.com/2023/01/sotol

Stephenson, N. (2018, February 23). *Mezcal: The "newest" old drink.* Paleoista. https://www.paleoista.com/food-and-drink/mezcal-keto-paleo-friendly

Sullivan, J. (2016, June 15). *Hibiscus mezcal and the art of a perfect infusion.* Tales of the Cocktail Foundation. https://talesofthecocktail.org/recipes/hibiscus-mezcal-and-art-perfect-infusion

Sweitzer-Lammé, M. (2022, August 16). *We asked 8 chefs: What's your favorite unexpected food and mezcal pairing?* VinePair. https://vinepair.com/articles/wa-food-mezcal-pairing/

Taxin, A. (2023, November 5). *California distillers turn to agave—but they're not allowed to call it mezcal or tequila.* Fortune. https://fortune.com/2023/11/05/california-distillers-grow-agave-spirits-not-tequila-mezcal-mexican-law/amp

Taylor, M. (2020, June 23). *When you drink mezcal every night, this is what happens to your body.* The List. https://www.thelist.com/218555/when-you-drink-mezcal-every-night-this-is-what-happens-to-your-body

Tequila.net. (n.d.). *What is a jimador?* https://www.tequila.net/faqs/tequila/what-is-a-jimador.html

Terrazas, F. (2023, March 6). *Fermentation.* Mas Mezcal. https://www.masmezcal.

com/mezcalvago/fermentation

The best mezcal deserves the best pairings: Here are our top 5. (n.d.). Mezcal Rosaluna. https://mezcalrosaluna.com/article/best-mezcal-pairings

The Crafty Cask. (2019, July 25). *Magical, misunderstood mezcal.* https://thecrafty cask.com/craft-spirits-liqueurs/mezcal

The Editors of Encyclopedia Britannica. (2023, December 12). *Oaxaca | History, attractions, economy, & facts.* Encyclopedia Britannica. https://www.britannica. com/place/Oaxaca-Mexico

The Insight Partners. (2023, October 11). *Mezcal market is projected to attain a size of $2.39Bn globally by 2030—Exclusive report by the insight partners.* Yahoo Finance. https://finance.yahoo.com/news/mezcal-market-projected-attain-size-133800871.html

The Lost Explorer Salmiana Mezcal. (n.d.). Spirits Kiosk. https://spiritskiosk.com/ the-lost-explorer-salmiana-mezcal

The Origins of Oaxaca Mezcal. (n.d.). Rosaluna. https://mezcalrosaluna.com/article/ origins-of-mezcal

The Producers: Geography. (n.d.). Great Agave. https://greatagave.com/geography

Thelmadatter, L. (2022, October 5). *Is Durango the next mezcal mecca?* Mexico News Daily. https://mexiconewsdaily.com/mexico-living/is-durango-the-next-mezcal-mecca

Theory, T. (2022, July 21). *What is tequila?* Uncle Julio's. https://unclejulios.com/ blog/news/what-is-tequila

Todd and Diane. (2011, April 8). *What is mezcal? Mezcal vs tequila from Mexico.* White on Rice Couple. https://whiteonricecouple.com/mezcal-mescal-alcohol

Tolstoy, L. (n.d.). *Leo Tolstoy Quotes.* Brainy Quotes. https://www.brainyquote.com/ quotes/leo_tolstoy_121890

Tomky, N. (2022, May 3). *Michoacán mezcal has arrived stateside—here's what to expect.* VinePair. https://vinepair.com/articles/michoacan-mezcal-american-arrival

Van Deventer, L. (2021, June 18). *The promises and pitfalls of Karoo agave.* Daily Maverick. https://www.dailymaverick.co.za/article/2021-06-18-the-promises-and-pitfalls-of-karoo-agave

Vasquez, M. (2021a, May 21). Everyone should know this about the designation of original mezcal. Agavache. https://agavache.com/everyone-shou

Vasquez, M. (2021b, June 21). *Terroir in mezcal?* Agavache. https://agavache.com/ terroir-in-mezcal

Velarmino, T. (2023, October 21). *Mezcal in Guanajuato: Mexico's mezcal region that we don't know about.* Mexico Insider. https://www.mexicoinsider.mx/mezcal-in-guanajuato-mexico

VinePair Staff. (n.d.). *How-to guide: Pairing spirits and food.* VinePair. https://vinepair. com/spirits-101/guide-pairing-spirits-food

Vorderbruggen, M. M. (2008, August 27). *Agave*. Foraging Texas. https://www.forag ingtexas.com/2006/05/agave.html#:

Wallace, D. (n.d.). *David Wallace Quote: "Fermentation may have been a better invention than fire"*. Quotefancy.com. https://quotefancy.com/quote/1712574/David-Wallace-Fermentation-may-have-been-a-better-invention-than-fire

Wally. (2022, September 26). *How Is mezcal made?* The Not So Innocents Abroad. https://www.thenotsoinnocentsabroad.com/blog/how-is-mezcal-made

Where Agaves Grow. (2022, July 26). Academia Patrón. https://www.academiapa tron.com/making-tequila/agave-growth-and-harvesting/where-agaves-grow

Wine Searcher Editorial. (2021, November 26). *Zacatecas mezcal and wine*. Wine Searcher. https://www.wine-searcher.com/regions-zacatecas

Wisniowski, J. (2022, February 15). *Oaxacan coffee recipe (tasty & authentic)*. Coffee Affection. https://coffeeaffection.com/oaxacan-coffee-recipe

Wolfe, P. (2023, January 30). *The surfer putting South African agave spirits on the map*. Tequila Raiders. https://tequilaraiders.com/article/leonista-south-african-agave-spirits-interview

Woodard, J. (2021, May 28). *Mezcal ranch water*. Dash of Jazz. https://www.dashof jazz.com/mezcal-ranch-water